the healing paw
not all angels have wings

Billy Roberts

Thorsor

Thorsons
An Imprint of HarperCollins*Publishers*
77–85 Fulham Palace Road,
Hammersmith, London W6 8JB

The Thorsons website address is: www.thorsons.com

Published by Thorsons 2000

1 3 5 7 9 10 8 6 4 2

© Billy Roberts 2000

Billy Roberts asserts the moral right to
be identified as the author of this work

A catalogue record for this book
is available from the British Library

ISBN 0 00 710949 0

Printed and bound in Great Britain by
Creative Print and Design (Wales), Ebbw Vale

Contents

Introduction   1
one | The Healing Nature   5
two | A Healer in Your House   11
three | The Psychic Profile   22
four | The Healing Process   31
five | Animals After Death   41
six | Extraordinary Animal Tales   48
seven | Pet Astrology   58
eight | Mystical Dog   71
nine | Meditating with Your Pet   76
ten | Man's Cruelty to the Animal Kingdom   83
eleven | The Wrong Programme   92
twelve | Cross My Paw With Silver   98
thirteen | Colour Power and Your Pet   102
fourteen | Growing to Look Like Your Pet   108
fifteen | Animal Magic   112
sixteen | The Holy Presence   118

Conclusion   123

Dedication

I dedicate this book to 'Harry' and 'Lucky' Roberts –
my canine friends

Introduction

Over the last 20 years or so a great deal has been written about the psychic abilities of animals but, as far as I am aware, little or nothing has been mentioned about the Healing Powers which animals undoubtedly possess. The therapeutic value of having a pet of any kind around the home is widely accepted today, and this theory has now extended to the practice of taking friendly furry canines to visit the elderly and infirm in hospices, homes and hospitals, in the belief that, 'A pat a day keeps the doctor away.'

P.A.T. dogs (Pets As Therapy) are proving extremely beneficial particularly in encouraging the recovery and rehabilitation of severely depressed patients, or those who have simply given up the will to live. In such cases, where perhaps the patient has ceased to communicate with those around them, the introduction of a friendly, gentle dog into the environment has often been instrumental in renewing the patient's interest in life. Those confined to nursing homes for the elderly also appear to derive great benefit from their P.A.T dogs, and each canine visit is eagerly awaited.

There is most certainly more at work here than the simple physical contact between human and animal. I firmly believe that there is a metaphysical side to the therapeutic value of animals, which has nothing whatsoever to do with the fact that the majority of them are furry, warm and cuddly.

Of course some animals are far from cuddly, but even they are still able to create an atmosphere of healing. One only has to consider, for example, the invaluable work done today with dolphins and sick and disabled children to appreciate just how special animals really are, particularly in the field of healing. It almost seems as though the dolphins know exactly what they are doing, as they swim and play with the small humans brought sometimes great distances especially to see them. And perhaps this is not so very far from the truth.

Some people though would appear to be completely untouched by the healing powers of animals. This would seem to be the case particularly when the person is not too fond of any kind of animal.

Some sort of emotional contact has to be established between human and animal before the healing process commences. However, the initiation of the healing process can be spontaneous and can take effect on the very first encounter, so it is therefore not necessarily dependent upon a long relationship. Taking time to stroke and speak to a friendly dog on the high street may be all that is needed to bring you relief from that niggling headache, or perhaps to lift that dark cloud of depression hanging over you, or to calm those taut nerves brought about by a stressful day. You have probably never put two and two together, and it has almost certainly never crossed your mind that the sudden disappearance of that awful headache had anything at all to do with that lovely old dog you patted outside the Post Office.

However, physical contact is not a prerequisite to receiving healing from an animal nor, I must add, is the ability to discharge healing confined to dogs alone. On the contrary, cats, birds, and many other species of animals have a pronounced healing effect upon the human organism. Nor is this healing force confined to domestic pets, for many wild animals too contribute to this healing atmosphere which is so necessary for man's spiritual, mental and emotional equilibrium. I will go as far as to say with certainty that man could not exist on a planet devoid of animals, for the Animal Kingdom contributes far more to the evolution of mankind than we know or are able to understand.

A leisurely stroll through the tranquillity of secluded woodland is most certainly therapeutic in itself, but the accompaniment of birds whistling and singing along our way most definitely introduces some other, more subtle, vibratory sensations to the experience. These vibrations have a profound effect upon both the mind and the emotions. I am not talking here about a simple experience of the auditory senses. This pleasant phenomenon goes far beyond that. For the musical harmonies of birds singing in the countryside create a healing veil of tranquillity which most definitely produces some sort of chemical change in the human brain.

Animals, like people, have a 'Psychic Profile'. There is far more to an animal than meets the purely physical eye.

Their personalities and characters also appear to be influenced by their astrological status, in much the same way as people. However, in the Animal Kingdom this influence is much more pronounced. For example, Capricorn and Cancer nearly always possess an inherent desire to care for others, and they are very often attracted to some sort of caring profession as a result.

In the Animal Kingdom this emotion seems to be much more pronounced, and those creatures born under these astrological signs create and release extremely vibrant healing forces into the environment. Of course this ability to discharge healing energy is far stronger in the creatures that interact with humans, such as family pets, as opposed to the wild animal.

In my exploration of the whole concept of the healing powers of animals I have come across many examples of the way in which humans have been positively altered, in one way or another, by this power. They are too much alike to be merely coincidence.

Although all animals possess some sort metaphysical force, to some greater or lesser degree, in this book we shall be concerned primarily with domestic dogs and cats, as they are closer to we humans than any other animal. Hopefully, when we have concluded our exploration of their Healing Powers, we shall have discovered a whole new meaning to the old saying

'A man's best friend is his dog.'

Author's note: There are times within the pages of this book where, in order to facilitate the flow of the text, I have been forced to refer to an animal as 'it'. I know that you, the reader, will forgive me.

one | **The Healing Nature**

It is all too easy to dismiss the healing abilities of animals, particularly when one is not too fond of them, but the truth is that more and more evidence is being presented to us today to substantiate the numerous claims that the presence of a furry creature in the home is good for the health of the whole family. In fact, it has now been scientifically proven that dogs and cats **are** beneficial to the health and that they do have a profound effect upon both the body and the mind. I am quite certain that most people will agree that when we are feeling a little sad and insecure, the warmth of our little furry friend is extremely reassuring and nearly always makes us feel a little better. Science is now telling us that this reassurance is not simply the result of warm fur against the skin. On the contrary, once we have allowed a dog or cat to interact into our family life, it usually discharges an extremely powerful force. This force can be scientifically measured and its effect upon the mind registered and monitored.

Over the past decade various studies have been made upon the effects animals have upon humans. The results of these studies show that those children who have been brought up with either a cat or dog are emotionally more receptive and far more sensitive than those who have not. A high percentage of the children brought up without a pet tended to be more aggressive in later life and often showed very little regard for animals.

However, it has also been argued that to be too passionate over animals can affect one's emotions and whole psychology adversely. In fact, those who dedicate their lives to fighting for the rights of animals often tend to live very unconventionally and occasionally choose to isolate themselves from the rest of society. A prime example is the French film actress Bridget Bardot who has become a recluse and now devotes her life entirely to animals.

It has always been my personal opinion that those who do not like animals at all lack something emotionally and very often appear cold; in fact, it was once said that those who do not like animals do not like people. Although this is not always the case, those who feel warm and loving towards other species are often more loving towards their own.

Cats and dogs exert great control over their owners and have an almost hypnotic effect upon them. For example, I am quite certain that every dog owner reading this has had the experience of sitting comfortably in front of the fire on a chilly autumn evening, when suddenly the thought 'What about Lucky's walkies' sprang into your mind, quickly followed by feelings of guilt. Try as you might, you simply cannot banish the thought from your mind and, as the minutes pass, the guilty feeling begins to irritate you. More often than not you give in to it, with thoughts such as 'Half an hour in the fresh air will do me good,' or 'It's only fair to the little chap'. So you stand up and call, 'Come on then, walkies!' Oddly enough, 99 times out of a 100, your little dog is already at the door, waiting to go.

You may think, as most people would, that the little creature has 'picked up' its master's thoughts telepathically – but you would be very wrong. For there is no doubt that the process of telepathy – that is mind to mind communication – is always in operation between a pet and its master, and more often than not, it is *your pet* who places the idea in your mind, not you!

Dogs and cats are constantly 'tuned into' the collective minds of the family and therefore can exert a powerful control over the entire household. They know instantly if a member of the family is unwell or the family as a whole is going on holiday.

Animals and people think in pictures. However, because man has evolved speech as a mode of communication, he tends to be under the assumption that he thinks with words – he does not! If I ask you to think of an elephant it is not the word *'elephant'* you see in your mind, but *the picture* of an elephant. This is processed at an incredible speed and then converted into the word. Animals do not have the same processing system, as their method of communication is far simpler and much quicker. They mentally transmit a series of pictures of what exactly they wish to say. Because of the rapidity of their thought transmission, animals are able to *know* what you are thinking long before your thoughts manifest as words.

So, the telepathic 'traffic' is not all one way, and although your dog is quite capable of *receiving* your mental intentions telepathically, it is also perfectly able to psychically *convey* to you its own desires and wishes. So to come back to that initial cold autumn evening, your sudden decision to take your pet for a walk was in fact *sent* to you by your furry little friend in subtle telepathic waves. Lucky was indeed one step ahead of you.

Although all animals possess healing properties in one form or another, it is the pets with whom we live who possess the greatest and most effective healing powers. Once a pet has established itself in a family environment, and is absolutely certain that it approves of everyone, it then sets about creating its own subtle atmosphere. This is perhaps the primary reason why a home bereft of animals is somehow not quite the same as one which possesses a furry presence. I am not talking about the sometimes pungent aromas, so familiar to all dog and cat owners, which those who do not have animals find most unpleasant. Nor am I talking about the discarded chews or a carpet of broken dog biscuits underfoot – common place things to pet owners. But rather there is another, more subtle force pervading the home of an animal keeper, and it is one that is immediately identifiable by another pet owner.

Those of you who share your homes with a dog or cat will understand exactly what I am referring to when I say, should your pet be absent from the home for 24 hours or more, you are able to 'feel' their absence in the subtle atmosphere of the house. There is an identifiable 'emptiness' in the atmosphere, which most of us find disquieting and even upsetting. It is almost as though animal lovers belong to some exclusive secret society.

There is very little doubt that animals do exert an extraordinary psychological hold on us and are able to aid our recovery from illness. I am convinced too, that we do not choose our pets. On the contrary, they choose us by consciously, telepathically drawing us towards them.

Once our pets have fully established themselves in the family environment, and that subtle atmosphere has been well and truly created, they then begin to attune themselves to each and every person in the household. Although a pet usually responds more to one particular person in the house (becoming known as either a man's or woman's pet) the animal itself *homes-in* on the whole family, weaving its mantle of authority over the entire household. Once a pet has been accepted as one of the family, life is never the same again.

To someone who loves dogs there is absolutely nothing in the world like the cuddle of this warm, loving creature. There is definitely an exchange of energies during such contact that has an incredible calming effect upon the human mind. However, this calming process is most certainly not restricted to physical contact. A lover of animals also experiences great delight in watching animals relaxing or playing. Healing of some sort is always experienced through any degree of mental interaction with animals. This healing process is not confined to animal lovers, for whether they are aware of it or not, people who do not particularly like animals are also affected by the healing created by animals.

In my exploration of the whole subject of animal healing, I have found that – where the degree and type of healing is concerned – there is a marked difference from animal to animal. Some dogs appear to have a remarkable effect upon illnesses associated with the nerves and emotions, whilst others appear to be extremely beneficial in aiding general recovery after illness. Whilst the healing abilities of dogs usually has nothing whatsoever to do with size or breed, the bigger, more fluffier dogs generally have an holistic effect upon the person, and have a profound effect upon the body and the mind thus promoting the self-healing process.

The healing force is not transmitted through any one part of a dog's body, but is somehow created by the whole personality, aura and physical presence. Therefore the healing process is not dependent upon touch (although contact facilitates the healing process) but merely being in the presence of some creatures for a length of time is really all that is needed. Evidence of this is seen when dogs are taken into homes for the elderly and infirm. In the presence of a canine visitor improvement is often seen in the overall appearance and behaviour of the person. The P.A.T. dog (Pets as Therapy) scheme has pioneered this discovery and rests on the very premise that elderly and infirm patients benefit from the company of dogs; because the results are extremely positive, the concept of P.A.T. dogs has been introduced as an alternative approach to the more traditional therapies. It does not really matter whether the recipient of healing likes dogs or not, they can still be affected. Dogs with the more gentle temperaments appear to have the most effective healing abilities and the healing process is most certainly helped a great deal when the dog has a pleasant disposition.

Although sceptics would say that our pets transmit this healing force unconsciously, I am not convinced that this is always the case. I would even go as far as to say that some canine and feline healers are totally aware of what they are doing, particularly when a close, loving relationship has been formed.

two | A Healer in Your House

Animals often use their psychic abilities to 'tune in' to their owners and through this ability they seem to know exactly when healing is needed. When a person is unwell, signals are sent out from their energy field, which a pet can easily sense.

When an affinity exists between a pet and owner, there appears to be a blending and harmonizing of their personal energies. The cat or dog is tuned in all the time to its owner's state of mind and it can therefore access at any time those feelings or emotions which indicate illness or anxiety. Having animals around the home is definitely good for the health and the deeper and closer the relationship one has with one's pet, the more healing is absorbed.

Although most people are oblivious to it, cats continually discharge waves of healing energy, either into the surrounding environment, or carefully targeted at a human. The contented, purring cat with arched back and tail held high, is a cat who is, often unknowingly, releasing its healing energies into the surrounding space. Anyone experiencing the pain of arthritis or rheumatism, or perhaps suffering from depression, should hold one hand a few inches above the tip a cat's tail, and then gently and slowly move it along to the head, without actually touching the cat. After this place your hand gently on your forehead for a few moments to effect some easing of the condition. This should be repeated several times – if your cat permits – in order to obtain some remarkable results.

Although all cats like to prowl, it is the one that does not stray far from home that possesses the most effective healing powers. Some cats appear to be very knowing and wise, and almost speak to their owners. These are the creatures with the strongest and most powerful healing energies, and they are the cats that have well and truly established that emotional bond with their owners. A psychic person would see the collective energies of this cat and its owner as one colourful mass, a perfect blend of colours, swirling one into the other.

Such a relationship between human and animal is quite common and the love one has for one's pet never goes unrewarded.

When your dog or cat senses that healing is needed it will gravitate towards its owner's bed of sickness and, once in close proximity, will not stray very far from that position. This is not just a simple show of affection on the part of one's pet – but an act of healing.

A dog's healing vibrations are less severe and a lot more subtle than a cat's. A dog's healing energies seem to be extremely effective on all sorts of illnesses. A loyal loving dog releases waves of healing, the effects of which are almost hypnotic, and can relieve many different kinds of pain almost immediately.

As I have mentioned previously, contact is not necessary for the healing process to take place. However, the healing powers of dogs and cats are far more effective on those with whom their personal energies have interacted. Once an emotional bond has been well and truly established between pet and owner, healing just flows from the furry creature to the part of the person's body where it is most needed.

There can be few things more stimulating, when one is feeling under the weather, than running one's fingers gently through your dog's fur, backwards and forwards, three or four times whilst you are relaxing beside it. After you have done this, it is good to simply sit quietly, with your hand gently resting on the back of your dog's neck. Of course, this sort of treatment is easier with long-haired breeds, but it is still possible with short-haired breeds. The facilitation of the healing process with short-haired breeds is initiated by gently stroking three or four times, from the head down to the tail.

Some breeds of dog possess far more potent healing powers than others. These powerful healing dogs are also often seen to have nicer temperaments and more loving dispositions than others. Larger dogs too tend to be better healers; but this is not to say that smaller dogs are not good transmitters of the healing force, they are, but they are not quite as strong as the larger dogs and the healing energy they emit is gentler.

One of the most powerful healing dogs is the Labrador. These dogs generally possess an extremely nice disposition and one might call them the gentlemen of the canine world. This is why they are so often used as guide dogs for the visually handicapped and as P.A.T. dogs.

The Labrador is an incredibly resourceful creature. It is patient to the extreme, and possesses enormously strong healing energies. Although very easy going, the Labrador is an extremely astute dog and very quickly attunes itself to its owner. Seen as a steadfast and loyal creature, the Labrador however often gives the impression of offering its friendship to anyone who is friendly towards it. Its open nature towards children ensures that its healing is especially suited for them. They are wonderful dogs to have around a family.

Labradors are extremely psychic and always appear to have a specific mission in life. The psychic profile of the Labrador is quite mystical, and reveals a profound spiritual connection between itself and man.

One of the most giving dogs is the Border Collie. This creature's healing abilities extend over a wide area, and they are extremely good dogs to have around the elderly or those people who are depressed or going through a traumatic period. Their healing emanations seem to have a profound calming effect upon the emotions, and just stroking or holding one close is often all that is needed to promote peace of mind and serenity.

Border Collies, whose ancestors were bred to work with sheep, seem to have somehow learned to proffer a paw as a show or an offer of friendship. I am quite certain that this action is something in-born in these dogs, and is most certainly a manifestation of their true sensitivity. Some years ago now I was fortunate enough to have a crossbreed Border Collie called Lucky. He was one of the most affectionate and loving creatures that I have ever had the privilege to know. I had been extremely ill for quite a long time, and often felt very tired and depressed. Whenever I was feeling at my worst Lucky always knew. He would stand in front of me and offer me the proverbial paw, and he would remain in that position, paw outstretched, until I took it. To encourage me to stroke him, Lucky would turn his back on me, and every time I stopped he would prod me with his nose until I stroked him again. Some people might say that all dogs do this in order to initiate being stroked. This is definitely not so.

Initially even I thought that Lucky simply wanted me to stroke him, as dogs usually do. But each time my hand touched him I was aware of a tingle in it, and a pleasantly warm sensation would pass from my hand and move up my arm to my chest. At that particular time I was suffering a lot of pain and my breathing was very laboured. I eventually noticed that everytime Lucky encouraged me to stroke him in this way my breathing gradually became easier, and the pain would fade. Once the worst of the condition had cleared Lucky appeared to know and he would then simply sit quietly beside me.

Lucky gave my mother similar 'treatment' when she was in a great deal of pain as a result of lumbago. Trying to find a comfortable position was a nightmare for her at that time. She tried the usual things – propping cushions behind her back, leaning to one side and then the other, but she rarely found much relief from the pain. On one occasion Lucky climbed onto my mother's chair and settled down behind her, and insisted on remaining stretched across her back, despite her protestations.

Strangely enough (as I thought at the time) my mother found some easement from the pain while Lucky remained close against her. I now know, of course, that Border Collies do have an amazing effect on painful conditions, and their friendly and gentle personalities exude a powerful calmness, which is extremely effective upon nervous and emotional conditions.

It is not necessary for the dog to be a pedigree in order for it to possess this healing force, for the healing ability is often found to be greater and more powerful in the humble mongrel.

Dogs are very much like people – their personalities vary from dog to dog. A grumpy dog may not be any the less a healer, but it may just not release the healing force as easily, or as pleasingly, as the mild mannered dog of pleasant disposition. I look upon animals as differently shaped people. They may not speak the same language as we do, but they certainly have their dreams, and think their own thoughts. The only difference is that they are not free to make their own decisions or able to live their own lives. Dogs and cats most definitely have their own opinions and often express them in ways that we do not as yet understand.

Today it is generally accepted that having animals around the home has a psychological and physiological effect upon our lives. Not only are our pets a great source of companionship, but their very presence in our lives somehow encourages a healthier mental attitude to life in general, thus promoting emotional, spiritual and physical equilibrium as a direct consequence.

For nine years I was privileged to share my life with an Old English Sheepdog called Harry. Unfortunately Harry died in 1998 aged nine. He was an extremely unusual dog who very quickly established himself in the family environment. It was very clear from the beginning that Harry was not only a wise dog, but even at the age of 12 months he appeared to exude a lot of love, which he was somehow able to transmute into healing, when it was needed.

From the tender age of three months old Harry offered a paw, which always remained in that position until it was taken. This might seem fairly commonplace to a lot of people – there is nothing unusual about a puppy offering its paw – once one 'gets to know' the little creature, the offering of the paw is seen to be, and experienced as, an expression of love and healing.

Harry, like other dogs, transmitted healing with just a brief encounter and appeared to have an extremely positive effect upon all those with whom he came into contact. Although Old English Sheepdogs are nearly all friendly and loveable creatures, they do not always transmit the same feelings, and some can be very unapproachable. I can only say from experience that Harry had the ability to relax me when I was tense, and stimulate me when I was feeling lethargic. I also noticed that Harry occasionally insisted on a cuddle. This was another way he effectively passed on his healing energies.

The fact that most animals possess specific metaphysical powers peculiar to the Animal Kingdom as a whole, has been known for thousands of years. In ancient Egypt for example, such powers were exploited in sacred healing rituals. Animals were called upon in special ceremonies to direct their mystical powers for all manner of reasons, some good: the wellbeing of humanity and the earth as a whole, and some purely bad: the furtherance of evil deeds.

In Egypt cats were principally used in ceremonies. They were looked upon with reverence and treated as a deity.

Cats are known to be very clean creatures. They are extremely resourceful, independent and quite particular. There has never been any question about their psychic abilities, and down the ages they have always been associated with witches and sorcery. They are very proud creatures, who often seem to feel that they have been placed on this planet with a specific mission in mind.

At best cats are extremely wise, at worst they can be sly and clumsy. However, they are of course very far from being stupid, and are, without a doubt, totally aware of their own capabilities and the powers they possess.

A cat's strong psychic powers enable it to influence the minds of its owners by sending them telepathic pictures in a subliminal way. The powers of a cat should never be underestimated, which is exactly why they have always been associated with witchcraft, and were known as a Witch's Familiar.

Whether you are a cat lover or not, holding one close to you is very much akin to holding an electrical dynamo. You can feel the magnetic power rippling through its lithe body. Accompanied by the feline's purring, this can have an extremely hypnotic effect upon the mind, helping you to relax.

The Elizabethans were only too aware of the healing properties of the cat, which they exploited to the full. Cats were often bred for their fur, which was draped over the bed in the winter months. This was not only done for the warmth of the fur, but also because Elizabethans believed that cat fur contained powerful healing properties which could ease the pain of gout and other inflammatory conditions.

The Elizabethan belief that the cat could cure a wide range of ailments was in fact sometimes carried to the extreme. The unfortunate feline's ears were sometimes cut off and the blood used to create a horrible concoction of vinegar, milk and honey. This they would drink, in the belief that this vile mixture would cure them of shingles and similar maladies of the nerves. However, I must say that this is certainly not recommended!

Some older folk still believe that their painful arthritic joints will be eased by allowing a cat to curl up on their lap, whilst relaxing in front of the fire. Unlike the Elizabethan theories, there is more truth in this theory than one might imagine.

Cats control their energies in completely different ways to dogs. As I mentioned earlier they are very much like small, powerful electrical dynamos, continually creating and discharging their vibrant force.

Remarkable changes occur in a cat's energy field when it is away from its home environment. Psychically the feline becomes like a kaleidoscope of swirling colour, with energy streaming from it. However, when it is in the comfort and safety of its own home its energy field becomes more quiet and serene. In fact, when a cat is seen relaxing in front of the fire, it discharges streams of vitality into the surrounding atmosphere.

You may like to try an experiment:

EXERCISE ONE

While your cat is stretched out in front of the fire kneel beside it and get yourself into a comfortable position. Place the fingers of both hands gently on your solar plexus.

With your eyes closed breathe in slowly and imagine yourself drawing in streams of white light through your nostrils. See this white light in your mind's eye, streaming into your lungs and then on into your solar plexus, from where it passes into your fingertips.

Hold your breath for a few seconds whilst moving your hands from your solar plexus to your cat. Then hold your hands over your cat, a few inches above its fur, with fingers outstretched. Then, as you breathe out, imagine the streams of white light pouring from your outstretched fingers into your cat.

Wait for it ...

Your cat will spring to its feet and, with arched back and tail held high in an 'S' shape, it should quickly move away from you.

The effect on your cat is in fact similar to that of an electric current passing through its fur. The breathing process creates an interaction of energy in the cat's body, causing a sudden surge of power through it. This will not harm your cat in anyway, but will simply prove to you that there is an energy force in your pet which can also be accessed and controlled.

All that your cat will experience is a sudden coldness, almost as though it has been splashed with icy cold water. You may even see its fur standing on end. In fact, this could be the ideal way of dealing with a disobedient cat.

This experiment does not work in the same way with dogs, because a canine's energies circulate through its body in a completely different way. However, if your dog is a little under the weather and perhaps not feeling too well, you can precipitate its own personal healing energies by applying the following procedure. Incidentally, **only** try this experiment if you are absolutely sure that you know your dog and that it is not given to bouts of aggression:

EXERCISE TWO

Sit comfortably, as close to your dog as possible. Place one hand on its nose, to secure it, and the other hand gently on its back.

If, for some reason or another, you do not like the idea of putting your mouth onto your dog's fur, place a small, clean, white linen cloth over the area before you begin the treatment.

Take a deep and full breath and then blow gently and slowly onto the top of your dog's head. Your lips should actually touch the fur (or cloth) firmly as you blow. Repeat this treatment five or six times.

Next, following the same procedure, blow gently into the back of your dog's neck. Repeat this process five or six times.

You may hear your dog grunting quietly with pleasure and its body become very relaxed and limp. Repeat the treatment three times a day until you notice some signs of improvement in your dog's condition.

This act of 'blowing' onto your dog actually stimulates its own healing processes into action, enabling self-healing to take effect. This is because the blowing technique infuses your dog with your own personal energy, which is strongest when expelled through the breath. I always found this extremely beneficial for my own dog, Harry, who suffered a great deal of pain in his hips and back legs. I would simply blow gently onto his back and hips for five minutes, then conclude the treatment by blowing gently onto the back of his skull. It always seemed to work for Harry and certainly eased his pain and made him very relaxed.

The technique of blowing gently onto animals is derived from an ancient Yogic method of healing which used to be practised on humans. Common sense must prevail here, and although this technique will work with cats, these creatures can be totally unpredictable and sometimes quite volatile, so blowing is not advisable where the feline is concerned.

When an animal is unwell they often lose quite a lot of their own personal vitality, so the actual process of blowing stimulates their central nervous system helping the movement of energy in their bodies. Once such movement has taken place, vitality is restored and the healing process encouraged.

three | The Psychic Profile

The extremely complex structure of the human subtle anatomy enables man to live a full and completely healthy life whilst residing in a physical body. It also allows him to access higher levels of consciousness and cosmic forces.

Man is much more than he appears at the physical level. He is far more than just a collection of cells which have a limited lifespan and then die. Rather, man is a powerhouse, whose psychic profile is in fact extremely complex. However, the complexities of man's subtle nature are a mere nothing in comparison to those of his animal friends.

We live in a multiplistic universe in which there are worlds within worlds. Each of these worlds rises in a gradually ascending vibratory scale, up to the extreme heights of the spiritual cosmos. Whilst man lives in a physical body he experiences some part of his existence in all these worlds at the same time, but is completely unaware of that fact. However, animals live out their innocent lives with the certain knowledge that they are cosmic beings, part of a larger whole; they perceive the universe in a completely different way than their human friends. Animals do not fear death in anyway whatsoever. They very often fear the cruelty and aggression shown to them by us humans, but death itself is viewed by the Animal Kingdom as being an extremely natural process of moving from one part of the universe to the other.

I have often said 'Not all angels have wings' *for it is my belief – as it is the belief of many others – that animals are the angelic beings sent to walk amongst us.*

Whilst the subtle or spiritual anatomy of animals is intrinsically the same as that of the human one, it is far more extensive in its nature. All the various species of animals on this planet are spiritually connected, one to the other, and work therefore in groups.

Some Christian schools of thought teach that animals do not, in any way, possess souls. This could be one way of them salving their consciences for the very fact that they consume animal flesh. Animals most certainly **do** have souls and in many ways are much greater and far closer to God than we humans.

These creatures, who live in close proximity to us and which we have taken into our families, play an extremely important part in our spiritual evolution. Such are the deep and profound feelings and messages that our family pets convey to us psychically, that they surpass speech and human understanding, and yet they have the power to emotionally and spiritually sustain us.

Although the intellectual qualities already developed in man have not as yet evolved in the Animal Kingdom, they have the potential to be as intellectually evolved as we are. One day the spiritual principles to which man is constantly aspiring, will be achieved by both the Human and Animal Kingdom. In my view some of the more gentle and intelligent creatures have already attained a significant spiritual status, and one only has to look at them to recognize their sensitivity and wisdom.

We are continually drawing in streams of cosmic energy which sustain us and help to perpetuate our life on this planet. Animals, too, are sustained in exactly the same way, but their metabolism transmutes this force in a more efficient way. Once the in-pouring energy has been transmuted and modified by their nervous systems, the residue of energy is immediately discharged into the surrounding space. Should the animal live in a loving, caring family environment, the vitality that it discharges is immediately coloured with the love the creature feels for its carers, thus affecting the whole family with healing.

People who love and like to be around animals draw into themselves quite a lot of vitality and are very often extremely sensitive and loving. Apart from having a deep fear of animals, or perhaps having some sort of allergic reaction to them, it is very difficult to understand why some people simply do not like animals at all. There are some people who carry their dislike of animals to the extreme and show a cruelty to them whenever they get the chance. Such people lack the sensitivity and inherent spiritual wisdom necessary to aid their own evolutionary processes.

Although there are exceptions, most people who love animals to the extreme nearly always seem to radiate an aura of gentleness and calm. Animal lovers are very often quite good at dealing with people with emotional problems and difficulties, and nearly always genuinely care for those less fortunate than themselves. Some animal lovers find it difficult dealing with other people's problems, and very often prefer the company of animals as opposed to people.

When a loving master is standing close to his dog there is an interaction of energies so that the aura of each of them manifests psychically as one.

Some animals have a very independent and slightly cautious nature. No matter how much love they are shown they never fully give themselves to anyone. This dog or cat always appears to have an air of arrogance and never really shows much affection to anyone.

As I have previously said, unlike humans, animals have total control over their personal energy fields and because of this they are able to manipulate the aura of their masters. When an animal is sending waves of healing to their master, all the nerves in its body seem to be vibrating as it begins to home-in – rather like the lens of a camera – on the person. Their whole energy field gradually expands, particularly around the face. The aura psychically extends outwards from the face in a spiralling stream until finally reaching its master. During this process the creature's owner usually experiences a warm rush of affection.

I am quite certain that some people will find this all a little too fanciful and perhaps far-fetched. However, in my experience this notion is very nearly always quickly dispelled when the following observations are made:

- Watch how your dog or cat behaves when you are unwell.
- When your dog is under the weather, see how it responds to the 'blowing' technique.
- When you decide to take your dog for its daily walk, notice what it is doing when the idea comes into your mind.
- When you are feeling extremely stressed hold your cat or dog close to you for a few minutes, and then see how you feel.

When a dog or cat is endeavouring to influence its master to do something in particular, its aura intensifies and its mental energies become focused with such force that a telepathic connection is established.

Both cats and dogs are quite proficient in transmitting mental signals, not only to humans but also to other animals. In fact, their method of communication seems to be universal with none of the language barriers experienced by humans. They also have the advantage of being able to access areas of the psychic world as yet unknown to man.

It is believed that before even the most rudimentary form of speech developed, man used to communicate his thoughts and feelings telepathically. Someone once said that speech was only developed so that man could tell lies. Whether or not research confirms this argument of one thing we can rest assured, the mind of the animal is finely attuned to every area of life. Furthermore, the animals who live with us in our homes closely monitor our actions and even our thoughts. Today dogs are being trained to use their monitoring skills to detect the onset of an epileptic seizure. It is possible for these sensitive canines to sense the approaching attack some hours before it actually takes place.

There are also dogs capable of 'sniffing' a cancerous condition in a person's body when the illness is otherwise difficult to diagnose. These creatures are so sensitive to the biological balance of the human body that they just 'know' when critical changes have disturbed the natural equilibrium, and things are not synchronized.

Cats possess greater streams of psychic vitality than dogs and they are able to transmute this force in a more powerful and direct way. Cats often create some sort of protective psychic force field around themselves, which can extend five to 10 inches beyond their normal auric field. Of course, this protective field is not always present, but is consciously created when the creature needs to defend itself from other animals or humans. The arching of the feline's back, and its hissing, do more than visually warn off predators. This threatening pose mirrors a change in the cat's psychic force – often perceived by other animals as bright shades of red. Once the cat calms down this shade of red is transmuted into a translucent shade of pink.

Whether or not one is able to view this phenomenon psychically, such a metamorphosis can be most certainly felt, as there is such an incredible release of energy from the creature at that time.

Although a dog releases a powerful surge of energy when it is angry or feeling threatened, it is not quite as demonstrative, because the in-flowing force in the canine is used up very quickly by its muscles, tissues, nerves and cells. A dog spends its energies much quicker than a cat, even though its metabolism is more sluggish. A cat will always gravitate towards a person who does not like cats, a dog usually avoids such a person.

Although animals have evolved a physiology which enables them to move far quicker and more nimbly than humans, their speed is also dependent upon the amount of energy force they are able to retain in their bodies. This force empowers the muscles to perform the almost impossible and enables the animal's performance to be perfectly synchronized to its psychological transmissions. For example, some wild animals are able to retain enough energy within their bodies that when they choose to release it they move so quickly as to appear as though their feet are not touching the ground. If it were possible for a human to perform physically as fast as his mind is able to think, he would have acquired incredible powers. The animal is almost capable of achieving such a phenomenon.

People who work a lot with animals are able, generally speaking, to shake off those minor ailments and infections that would force most of us to take to our beds. Those who work in dog and cat sanctuaries develop, after a time, a strong intuitive relationship with the creatures in their care. These people often find that their senses and general awareness are sharpened and become somehow more acute, simply as a result of being constantly around animals. Vets, too, are affected in the same way, and are very often able to intuitively diagnose health conditions.

Animals do give us far more than we know or are able to understand. Having been brought up in a family that always had a dog in the home, I know only too well that animals do contribute a great deal to the emotions of a growing child. In fact, I feel that all children should be given the opportunity to get to know animals, and should be allowed, if at all possible, to have a pet.

Animals most definitely respond to affection and will always reciprocate any love given to them. Some people find it much easier to express their feelings to a family pet than to another person. Animals are easier to understand than people and can be relied upon without fear of betrayal.

Believe it or not, animals do have emotions, dreams and opinions. They are extremely good judges of character so, if your dog does not like a person then, believe me, you should seriously consider their displeasure as being a definite warning about the person's true character. In fact, the awareness and sensitivity of your family pet extends much further than you might imagine. Not only is your dog able to put ideas into your mind, but it may come as a surprise to learn that it can also 'hear' your thoughts, long before they have actually manifested in your consciousness.

I have always found it difficult to believe that there are people on the planet who simply do not like animals. However, we cannot ignore the fact that not everyone likes animals. Often the person who simply cannot stand cats or dogs is lacking in cosmic vitality, the principle primarily responsible for the subtle manifestation of emotion and sensitivity. These people are quite often prone to depression and can be quite irritable, moody and sometimes volatile. These people are 'out of tune' and animals can quite easily pick up on it.

People show their dislike of animals in various ways of course. They may scowl, move away from the animal, push it away from themselves, or simply ignore it completely. But whichever way the displeasure is shown, whether overtly or not, a subtle scent is released from the person and the animal immediately smells it.

When faced with a human who simply does not like them, each dog and cat will deal with the dislike in a different manner. Some dogs can be extremely hurt, they obviously expect everyone to love them as much as their owners do. Friendly loving dogs just cannot believe it when they meet somone who does not like them, and they find it quite difficult to accept.

There are two kinds of dogs: the first kind will always give the stranger the benefit of the doubt, and will offer the paw of friendship, so to speak, on the first meeting. However, should that paw not be accepted in the manner it was offered the dog will move away with a look, which says 'I get the picture, you've had your chance pal, but I live here and you don't'.

Thereafter this dog will keep well away from the unfriendly person and, in the future, will use every endeavour to make them feel uncomfortable.

The second sort of dog is more the 'go in and ignore it ' kind of dog. This canine will often appear oblivious to a visitor's discomfort, and will lie at their feet, or sit as close as possible to them, seemingly in an effort to receive some sort of stroke of approval, or perhaps even a tummy rub, or just a smile. Very few people can fail to be touched by this approach. The emanations of healing vitality that a dog will direct will soften their displeasure. Even the staunchest of animal dislikers will eventually find themselves glancing across at the creature, or even (heaven forbid!) reaching out and stroking it.

Cats deal with the problem of a human who dislikes them in a completely different way. For some reason – best known to themselves – cats always target a disliker, even in a room full of people. Perhaps a cat knows, more than any other creature, that the person who dislikes it is badly in need of something it possesses a lot of – healing vitality. So it sets about passing some on, even though this thoughtful action may make it even more unpopular.

The cat will approach the disliker's legs, slowly at first, to check how the land lies. Then, purring, it will move in close and rub its body against first one leg then the other. It will give each leg two or three treatments before moving up to the person's lap, where it usually curls into a ball, resisting most attempts to move it. There is definitely no escape for the person who does not like cats!

four | The Healing Process

Dogs and cats discharge their subtle waves of healing vitality while appearing to simply be expressing pleasure or greeting others. A dog will wag its tail and wiggle its bottom, while a cat will arch its spine and raise its tail into an 'S' shape. Although most of us miss the release of healing and perceive the animal to be merely being friendly, those who are psychic would see the release of energy as shimmering vibrations – rather like electricity, completely surrounding the creature in a fan-like shape.

Whereas the cat releases most of this force from its tail, the dog discharges it predominantly from its head and sometimes its back. However, a dog possesses great amounts of this vitality in its rear end and the simple act of stroking its back down to its bottom precipitates a powerful release of energy. This process is extremely beneficial when one is feeling unwell or just a little run down. Not only does it have a calming effect upon the mind, but also it often has the effect of anaesthetizing the body to pain.

Although the healing vitality of the feline and canine is to be found in the fur of both creatures, it is in fact more prevalent in the fur of the cat. Some schools of thought believe that there are nine degrees of animal healing vitality in the supersensual universe, and the cat is the only creature on the planet whose fur contains these nine degrees. Hence the saying 'a cat has nine lives.'

This subtle healing vitality is not peculiar to the animal kingdom alone. On the contrary, some humans possess it in great amounts, and these people have the ability to heal through the laying on of hands.

Cats are able to transmute this vitality into a potent force and as a result they are nearly always able to evade death when they find themselves in the most dangerous and precarious of situations. Dogs are not so fortunate; as a direct result of the sluggish way in which their vitality circulates around their bodies, they are often quite slow in dangerous situations.

The highly volatile nature of a cat's healing vitality is a key reason for felines' adversity to water. Placing a cat in water is like placing two opposing magnetic forces together. You can produce the same effect if you take a deep breath and slowly blow onto your fingertips, then - holding your hands over your cat's back - shaking them vigorously. The cat will immediately arch its back, its tail will rise into an 'S' shape, and it will quickly move away from you.

This reaction is the result of the interaction of two opposing forces which, quite obviously the cat finds unpleasant. Most dogs, however, find the experience quite pleasant and will often come back for more. This is primarily because the dog's energies are not quite as vibrant as a cat's, and they manifest in a completely different way.

The healing power of animals is all the greater when there is more than one pet in a household. Hopefully their energies will be compatible, in which case the animals will often relax in a huddle. (This behaviour is especially pronounced if there are multiple dogs in a home.) Their combined energies create a sort of powerful 'Healing Battery' giving off incredible heat, both physically and psychically. Anyone in the house suffering from arthritis or rheumatism will derive great benefit from this healing force – without realizing that it has anything at all to do with the hairy huddle in front of the fire.

Both dogs and cats in multi-animal households pass on the healing force to each other, and when one of the group is feeling unwell it may move close beside another, in an effort to have its low levels of vitality restored. Animals are natural healers and only have their levels of vitality lowered either when they are unwell, or when they have been injured. In the latter case it is shock, a condition that often follows an injury, which causes a spontaneous loss of vitality in the animal.

Sickness creates a subtle fragrance that is perceptible to animals. The degree of fragrance informs them about the seriousness of the illness. Cats, especially, like to cuddle close to a sick person and they most certainly contribute a lot towards their recovery. Although it is a known fact that cats like heat, and so are therefore attracted to the heat of a person's body when there is a fever, they also do this in an asserted effort to aid the invalid's recovery.

Recently I was told the sad story of an elderly widow's nine year old Jack Russell dog which had always slept in her bedroom. However, when she took to her bed with an incurable illness he refused to go upstairs to be beside her. Only after the lady passed away did the little dog go into her room and lay beside her on the bed, crying.

It would appear that the Jack Russell simply could not bear to watch its mistress so ill and in pain. Many dogs feel helpless when their owners are gravely sick and such acts of emotion are in fact much more common than one might imagine.

Whenever your dog is a little under the weather, you can encourage the self-healing process by stimulating its powerful healing energies through the use of a number of different techniques.

TECHNIQUE 1

Place your dog in a position which enables you to gain easy access to its spine. Using your right hand, with the fingers loosely outstretched, simply shake your fingers quickly and energetically whilst moving your hand slowly down your dog's spine – from the base of the skull to the tip of the tail.

Repeat this process, over and over, for five minutes, occasionally pausing to blow warm breath into your fingertips. When blowing into your fingertips, try to imagine that you are infusing them with a powerful white energy. In fact, see this energy vividly in your mind, passing from your mouth to your fingertips. Try to feel your fingers almost alive with vitality.

Next, simply stroke your dog slowly along the spine, following the same route as before, to encourage the healing force to move. Once you have completed the exercise you should see your dog become relaxed and it will probably go to sleep.

TECHNIQUE 2

Blow gently into the top of your dog's head for a few minutes. Then rub the area softly with your fingertips to encourage the energy to move. Next, move to the base of the skull and gently blow into it for a few moments. Again, rub the area gently.

Continue this blowing technique along the route of your dog's spine, concluding at the base, just before the tail.

It is a good idea to use a white linen cloth during this process as the white linen helps to retain the warmth created by the blowing, and this warmth is essential in the precipitation of the healing vitality. Because dogs have so much vitality in their bodies, the blowing process is extremely effective in encouraging self-healing.

This technique may be practised on humans who will also find it greatly beneficial, particularly in those cases involving a great deal of pain.

You can use different coloured pieces of linen depending on the degree and nature of the illness:

Red linen will infuse the vitality from your breath with strength and power. It is extremely beneficial in the healing of blood conditions and for lifting feelings of lethargy.

Orange linen is extremely effective where there are digestive problems, or when there is a lack of appetite accompanied perhaps by tiredness.

Yellow linen will aid the stimulation of the major glands and organs of the body and is extremely beneficial in the healing of kidney or urinary problems.

Green linen has a remarkable effect upon the heart and will also aid the recovery from emotional or psychological trauma.

Blue linen will aid the process of relaxation and will also help to promote equilibrium between the body, mind and spirit.

Indigo linen seems to have a general toning effect upon the body and the mind. It is also beneficial in aiding recovery from serious illness.

Violet linen tends to have an holistic effect upon the body and is extremely effective in treating cancerous conditions.

Remember, though, it is not the linen that does the healing, as much as the infusion of the colour and the vitality from your own body. Once the breath reaches the coloured linen, your vitality immediately becomes infused with the appropriate colour rays, the combination of which has a powerful effect upon the condition you are treating.

Although this book is primarily concerned with the healing powers possessed by animals, it is equally important to understand the ways in which these powers can actually be used to heal the animals themselves when they are ill. Your pets are little powerhouses on four legs, and they possess the ability not only to heal you, but also to heal themselves.

Dogs more than cats appear to respond to the healing vibrations of colour, and certain colours may be used around your pet to encourage the healing of specific illnesses. For example, should your dog be hyperactive, and forever on the go, put a pink sheet or cover on its bed. Pink is an extremely calming colour and its vibrations will not only help to calm your furry canine, but they will also promote restful sleep.

If your pet is suffering from a high temperature, give it a blue blanket to sleep on. The vibrations of the colour blue will help to reduce the temperature and, as your pet is not susceptible to suggestion, there is no question of a placebo effect. Colour treatment can be quite effective, and in a lot of cases extremely powerful.

The elderly dog who is suffering perhaps from a tired or diseased heart will quite often benefit from treatment involving the colours green and blue. Allow your pet to rest for a while on a green cover or sheet bathed, if possible, in a green light. Then change the cover to a blue one, bathed in a blue light. Of course this treatment must be applied over a number of weeks, in order to obtain the desired results.

Just as one would expect the colour blue to reduce a higher than normal temperature, the colour red will raise it when your pet is suffering from a chill and has a low temperature. Allow your little invalid to rest for half an hour or so on a red cover, and bathe it in a red light for just fifteen minutes. Results should be seen quickly with this colour, because red carries a great deal of energy with it, and has a tendency to create a lot of heat in a physical organism. It is also an extremely effective colour in the healing of arthritis. Arthritis may also be induced by hip replacement, which should be treated with the colour red and – because in there can be inflammation – the colour blue.

Generally speaking yellow is a stimulating colour and can be very effective when treating health conditions that result in fatigue and lethargy. But yellow is also useful when treating stomach, bowel or kidney conditions. Treatments using the yellow vibration will be greatly strengthened when concluded with a short period of green, for this is the colour of harmony and equilibrium.

Animals suffering from a terminal illness can often have their pain and discomfort reduced greatly by treating them with the colours purple and blue. As before, allow your pet to lie on a bed of purple for 30 minutes and if possible bathe it in a blue light for a further 15 minutes. Then reverse the process and allow your pet to rest on a bed of blue to be bathed if possible in a purple light. This treatment will not cure the condition but it will certainly help to alleviate and ease the suffering.

Dogs are naturally drawn to nature and therefore benefit from, and greatly appreciate, a regular walk in the countryside or park. Nature's colours are so important to the Animal Kingdom and the colour green in particular is vital to a dog's mental and emotional equilibrium. Just to feel the cool grass beneath its paws is a tonic in itself. Dogs love to roll over on the grass – not only does this feel nice and cooling on their bodies – but it also recharges their systems with energy and vitality. In fact, we humans could learn a great deal from our dogs, who seem to know exactly what to do, and how to do it, to restore their vitality.

My Old English Sheepdog, Harry, used to love to roll over in the freshly dug earth of the vegetable patch, to my family's horror and his delight. Then he would lie flat out and motionless in it, for anything up to 20 minutes, after which time he would demonstrate an energetic marathon running around the garden. It was obvious that his sojourn in the vegetable patch did more for him than just cool him down in warm weather. To see Harry psychically when he emerged from the broccoli stems was quite a sight to behold. Sparks of electricity appeared to be radiating from him and he would almost glow with power. Holding him close and giving him a cuddle at that time was quite invigorating. I could feel his energy vibrating through me, perhaps like being plugged into an electrical generator!

Like humans, animals derive most of their vitality from the air and the sunlight. Water tends to be an excellent conductor of the vitality necessary for the maintenance of the health in the physical body. Water is also a cleansing agent and has a purifying effect upon the organs of the body and the blood. Water may be infused with a specific healing colour ray with the following procedure. This technique can also be used in the treatment of human ailments, but animals somehow respond to it a lot quicker.

EXERCISE THREE

For this treatment you will need to obtain a number of sheets of A4 acetate, in as many different colours as possible. Make each piece into a tube by Sellotaping or stapling them ensuring that they are large enough to fit over a glass tumbler.

The object here is to filter the natural vitality coming into the water and by introducing a specific colour ray into the process, you thus increase the vitality level in the water. The appropriate filter is simply placed over a glass of water, which is then placed on a window ledge in the bright sunlight, preferably outdoors.

Leave the tumbler exposed to the sunlight for at least an hour. After this time, pour the water from one tumbler to another, backwards and forwards to revitalize it. When you have completed this process pour it into your dog's bowl. It is a good idea to prepare a few tumblers so that there is enough for a few doses. Should the water remain in the bowl for any length of time, revitalize it occasionally so that it does not lose its taste.

When using the filters it is important to use your imagination and instinct when selecting the appropriate colours. I have already said that red is a powerful colour that tends to create heat in the physical body. It will help to raise the temperature when it is low. Blue is quite the opposite and will lower the temperature when it is high. Blue also calms the nerves when there is anxiety or stress. Please see pages 35–38 for examples of the healing properties of different colours.

At the beginning of this book I said that *'A cuddle a day keeps the doctor away.'* I would now like to add to that *'A cuddle a day keeps the vet away.'*

Cuddling or stroking your dog as a show of affection releases a lot more than physical warmth. There is definitely a more subtle process at work here – an exchange of energy that has the power to heal human illnesses of both the body and the mind and to sustain and prolong the life of both the human and the animal.

The only gift that your pet expects from you, is the gift of love.

five | Animals After Death

There is little doubt that once a pet has well and truly established itself in the home it becomes one of the family. Having a furry presence in the house contributes something to the overall atmosphere. Only an animal lover can be privy to those almost sacred feelings that are passed on to anyone who belongs to this elite group of 'animal people'.

This may well sound quite absurd to those who do not love animals and that is exactly the point I am trying to make. For when a little creature captures one's heart some sort of magical transformation takes place in the emotions, and life, believe me, can never be the same again.

An animal lover seems to undergo some sort of secret initiation into the club of *silly talk*, 'walkies ... din-dins ... Who's mummy's little soldier?'. And of course our faithful little friend understands every word.

Little wonder then when the inevitable happens, and that little furry presence dies, either through age, illness, or the worst scenario – a car accident – the grief is just as painful and unbearable as that of losing any other member of the family. In fact, to some people it is quite often worse.

Coming to terms with the loss of a pet can be extremely difficult, and for an elderly person living alone, painfully sad, as they bid farewell to a constant, loving companion. 'Replacing' a pet, or even just thinking of 'replacing' it generates often unbearable feelings of guilt. It is commonly felt that to replace a pet with another creature, even some considerable time after their death, would be disloyal, and would cause some sadness and jealousy to the pet that has died. It is often strongly believed that the little creature may be looking on from that part of the Spirit World where animals go when they die.

But where exactly *do* animals go when they die? Do they go to the same place as humans? Is there a Heaven and a Hell for animals? Do their lives continue in the same way as humans' lives in the Spirit World?

At death the spiritual essence of the animal is released, enabling it to gravitate towards that sphere of light where all animals reside. Strictly speaking, there are no evil animals and therefore no plane of existence that could be defined as 'Hell'.

The aggressive creature does not choose to be aggressive and has no control over its aggression. Unlike the human the animal does not possess a conscience, so it therefore cannot be considered guilty of any misdeed. Although some domestic animals do exhibit some form of rudimentary conscience, at this stage of their evolutionary process, no animal can be held responsible for its actions.

All creatures great and small do live on beyond death. Although the more advanced animals retain their individual personalities at death, their evolutionary processes continue in the collective sense. All animals develop spiritually, emotionally and intellectually through the group soul.

To think of your pet dog or cat as being merely a small part of a greater soul might seem a little disappointing. However, anyone who truly loves and understands animals will fully comprehend this concept. In fact, it will enable them to see exactly why the Animal Kingdom as a whole has such a great and powerful influence over mankind.

Ridiculous as it may sound to some people, the family pet feels a sense of responsibility towards its owner, especially when it has been a part of an extremely close and loving relationship. And it is this sense of responsibility and concern which draws it back to the family home after it has died.

One of the most common experiences pet owners have when their cat, dog or any pet dies, is to continue to'feel' them around the home. In a lot of cases they may even be fleetingly seen sitting on their favourite chair, or perhaps curled up in their favourite corner. These experiences transcend the bounds of coincidence and imagination because far too many people have had astoundingly similar experiences.

Even though the owner may not always be aware of the furry creature's presence, just being around the home allows the pet to continue its own personal development, as well as enabling it to further enjoy those wonderful waves of love created by the family. This love is so important for the spiritual evolution of animals and without it the animal kingdom as a whole would be unable to function and grow.

In the Great Spiritual Universe the various species of which the Animal Kingdom is collectively composed occupy their own individual stratum of existence, but the same spiritual bond that unifies the whole of creation unifies these species. The various strata of existence upon which all animals have their being are tended by a group of highly evolved souls who together have sole charge over the Animal Kingdom. Very few of these exalted beings have ever had a physical existence and those amongst them who have, have become known on earth for their kindly and compassionate works towards animals. Saint Francis, amongst others, is one such being and his name is now synonymous with the care and love of animals.

A dog or cat who has interacted into family life and has become attuned to, and very much a part of the family, has usually evolved an almost human-like intelligence and knowing nature. It needs therefore to come back often from the spirit world, not only to imbibe the family love and to make quite sure that everything and everyone is alright, but also to offer some reassurance to the family of their own continued existence after death. An animal that has been treated with love and kindness will never forget, and will always take every opportunity to return to those who have given them so much love.

On the other hand, animals that have been treated cruelly never bear any malice or seek revenge on those who have inflicted so much pain and misery upon them. The perpetrators of such cruelty towards innocent creatures have a flaw in their own spiritual natures and are eventually punished by their own cruelty. Nothing in creation ever passes by unnoticed, for the same spiritual laws that operate in the Great Spiritual Universe are also in constant operation in the physical world.

All animals on earth are the ambassadors and representatives of those spiritual beings who silently and relentlessly watch over and guide mankind.

It may or may not come as a great surprise to pet owners to learn that they have an *angel* in their home. Believe me, not all angels have wings. If you truly love your pet you will understand exactly what I mean.

Animal Reincarnation

Those creatures who live alongside humans are born with a specific mission to fulfil. Each one is spiritually linked to the others of its species, collectively forming the *soul*. Therefore, once each creature has reached a specific phase in its spiritual evolutionary development, the whole group is then recalled to be subjected thereafter to the process of reincarnation.

The doctrine of re-birth forms an integral part of some religious teachings, especially Eastern religions such as Buddhism. However, reincarnation in the Animal Kingdom is very different, and far more complex, than that of humans.

Animals in Eastern religions are often used as 'vehicles of transgression'. For example, man may be reborn into the body of an animal should he perform some grave misdeed, or perhaps be cruel to an animal or even kill one unnecessarily. The concept of 'Transmigration of Souls', that is being reincarnated into the body of an animal as a punishment for our sins, is a belief embraced by some Eastern cultures.

In the process of re-birth animals are mostly born in groups and not always as the same species. Collectively they make up the group soul that works towards the fuller development of the Animal Kingdom as a whole. This group soul is continued into life, where although separated in a physical sense, they maintain a telepathic connection.

Should a domesticated animal form a close bond with a human they may disconnect from the group, at least for a short while, in order to continue, and deepen, its relationship with the owner in a different body. Such are the connections between some pets and their owners that they are reborn immediately after death. This is in an asserted effort to comfort the grieving family through the guise of another creature. One such account was given to me by Agnes, an elderly lady who claims that her grief over the death of her 14 year old King Charles Spaniel, Tara, forced her faithful companion to return to her in the body of another dog.

The very thought of 'replacing' Tara with another dog appalled Agnes. So, when her son Michael brought her a six-week-old cross Border Collie, she could not contain her anger, telling him to take the puppy away at once. Michael persuded his mother, after some time, to 'give it a try'.

As soon as the little dog was placed on the living room floor to roam freely around, it went straight over to Tara's toy box. You may think that there is nothing very surprising in that, but in fact Tara's toy box was neatly and completely hidden in the corner of the room, behind the bookshelves. Having joyfully and noisily examined Tara's old toys, the puppy then followed its curiosity into the kitchen and straight to the spot where Tara's water bowl had stood for many years. There it waited until Agnes placed a saucer of water in front of it.

In fact the little dog appeared to have far more than a superficial knowledge of the house, its contents and its layout. This became more and more apparent as the days went by, and her new companion's behaviour quickly convinced Agnes that Tara had returned to her in a different body.

I also heard the heartbreaking story of a little boy's love for his seven-year-old Labrador, Blackie. Daniel was best friends with Blackie and they spent most of their time together when Daniel was not at school. The heartache began when Blackie was knocked down and killed by a taxi while on his way along the road to meet Daniel from school.

Devastated by Blackie's death, Daniel became withdrawn and depressed and would not eat. As a result, in only a very short time, he became quite poorly. Desperately worried about Daniel's deteriorating health, his mother took him along to a nearby animal shelter, in the hope of encouraging her son to show an interest in another dog. Although, as she told me, she thought this highly unlikely, she wanted Daniel to be happy again and was prepared to try just about anything to that end.

However, to her complete surprise, Daniel's eyes lit up with delight as soon as he saw a small white West Highland Terrier standing alone in one of the pens. He pleaded with his mother to allow him to take the little dog home, insisting that it was in fact Blackie, his Labrador. But, as the West Highland Terrier had been alive at the same time as Blackie, there was no possible chance for them to be one and the same dog.

Nevertheless, Daniel was insistent, and had intuitively recognized something deeper and more profound in the little dog. Whatever this was, his mother could see that Daniel really did believe that his beloved Blackie had returned to him.

The 'new addition' quickly settled in to his new home, behaving almost as though he had always lived there. The terrier moved around the house with confidence and with an almost uncanny knowledge of where everything was situated.

Daniel speedily recovered his health and his mother was delighted to see him happy again. Blackie installed himself as the family pet and became, of course, Daniel's new best friend.

six | **Extraordinary Animal Tales**

Over the last few years, in response to several appeals I have made for information, I have amassed a huge collection of true stories concerning the healing abilities of animals. Some of these stories are genuinely amazing. It is clear to me that although most people can find no explanation for their own particular 'pet' experience, there is a general acceptance that animals do possess powers that humans, as yet, do not fully comprehend.

It would seem also that the healing powers that animals possess can extend from beyond the grave. There are many stories to corroborate this and to illustrate that the love a pet (dogs in particular) has for its owner survives physical death. It is this great force that can be instrumental in promoting a person's recovery from illness.

To dogs and cats the spirit world and the physical world are seen as one. They perceive the inhabitants of the spirit world with the same clarity as they do those living about them in the physical world; animals still possess this deeply profound, although primitive, awareness that humans once possessed but which have long since lost.

Cats can often be seen playfully clawing at the air, endeavouring to make contact with something that is completely invisible to the human physical eye. Dogs too are often seen moving their gaze slowly around the room, intently watching something that we cannot see.

It has become common knowledge over the years that animals often see things that we cannot. They live, in fact, between two worlds, and are able to see two completely different landscapes, one super-imposed upon the other.

Animals are able to have much more than just a superficial contact with the spirit world. They are able to continue a loving relationship should their owner die and 'leave' them. Here are some stories of owners and their pets whose love and devotion for each other went beyond the grave.

Bess was an old Labrador and Len Oates' constant companion since the death of his wife three years before. Man and dog had developed a very special relationship in which (Len swore) each knew exactly what the other was thinking. Len would speak to Bess as though she were human and he knew that she understood his every word. Bess was obedient, loving and loyal, and very rarely strayed far from her doting master's side. Len had come to rely on her more and more since his heart attack 18 months before. They went everywhere together, and on the odd occasion when Len left Bess at home, she would always be waiting for him at the window on his return. Bess loved her three outings each day on the common across the road, and hail, rain or snow Len never disappointed her.

Four days before Christmas Len was in bed suffering from the 'flu, so the job of walking Bess had been handed to Len's next door neighbour, a kindly lady who looked in on him several times a day.

On their return from the common Bess collapsed and died. Of course Len was absolutely devastated and did not know how he would be able to face life without his dearest friend. Over the weeks that followed Len fell into a deep depression and, deprived now of his reason to go out every day, he refused to set foot over the doorstep. He cut himself off from everyone. He stopped eating and eventually could see no point in going on. Len became so ill that his only daughter came from the South of England to stay with him.

One night whilst lying in bed unable to sleep, just staring sadly into the darkness of his room, Len suddenly heard a shuffling sound beside his bed. Before he could move a weight settled on his feet. Peering anxiously through the dim light to the end of the bed Len simply could not believe what he saw there: Old Bess was lying stretched across his feet, just as she had always done.

Convinced that he was dreaming, Len sat forwards to stroke Bess and was instantly shocked to feel her warm, familiar fur. Bess immediately stood up and scrambled along the bed towards him. With tears streaming down his face Len put his arms around her and hugged her. He knew this was no dream. Bess was 'alive' and warm and sitting in front of him. But, after only a moment, she jumped down from the bed and faded away into nothingness as Len watched.

When he woke the next morning Len felt like a new man. His daughter was surprised when she came into the kitchen to find him already washed and shaved, and ready to take an early morning walk across the common, something he had not done since Bess's death. For Len now knew that Bess would always be there somewhere by his side and he had no intention of disappointing her. 'She's alive!' he told me. 'She's alive somewhere, and I know we'll be together again someday.'

Most people, no matter how much they have loved their pet, are not lucky enough to experience what Len experienced. Bess somehow managed to manifest to him, most probably because she knew just how ill he had become following her death. Her appearance certainly had a hugely positive effect on Len, both emotionally and physically.

Grace Johnson had been blind from birth. Until recently her 'eyes' and constant companion had been Polly, a black Labrador who had been with Grace since she was a pup. Theirs was a very close and loving relationship. But, at 12 years old, Polly had been put to sleep because of an incurable growth in her stomach.

Grace was devastated, but had been extremely fortunate to get another guide dog, Buster, so quickly. Also a Labrador, he was a nice pleasant dog, but he was not Polly. Polly had known Grace's every move and, of course, poor Buster did not. It was almost as though Polly had known exactly what Grace was thinking. She had somehow been attuned to Grace's every need and had looked after her when Grace had felt unwell.

Although an animal lover and a lover of dogs in particular, Grace did not seem to have the same rapport with Buster. It did not help either that when they were out walking together in the street Buster made mistakes and hesitated in heavy traffic. Grace now had little confidence in Buster's ability to guide her safely when they went outdoors.

Grace's thoughts turned often to Polly with deep sadness. She wanted so much to love Buster in the same way, to trust him, and to look upon him with confidence, as she had with Polly – but she could not.

Time passed, and the situation showed no signs of improving. When Grace was at her lowest, depressed and trying desperately to decide what to do with Buster for the best, something very strange happened.

She was on her way with Buster to the Post Office in the town centre when she noticed, to her surprise, that he was behaving quite calmly and doing everything just as he should. He seemed almost like a different dog, as though it was Polly – not Buster – leading her. The transformation had been so sudden that Grace was completely taken aback. When they arrived home and Grace settled herself in the armchair by the fire, Buster surprised her again by sitting close beside her, something he had never done before, usually preferring to stretch out in front of the fire.

The marked change in Buster's behaviour pleased Grace and she could suddenly feel warmth from the dog, almost as though he had really begun to care for her. In fact Buster continued to improve as the days went by and Grace and he began to develop a close, loving relationship. It was not until the local vicar called to see her that Grace realized why her dog's behaviour had changed so suddenly and dramatically.

The vicar was not aware that Polly had died and during his visit he remarked to Grace how nice it must be for her to have two dogs escorting her to the shops. Assuming that Polly was nearing retirement age, he said how touching it was to see her 'training the new dog'. When Grace told him that Polly had been gone for over five months and that Buster was her new companion, the vicar simply could not believe it.

Grace continued to feel Polly's healing touch around the home for quite some time, even after Buster had learned the ropes and settled in. Buster became Grace's trusted companion and invaluable 'eye'.

Humans are not alone in having paranormal experiences – if they could talk they would surely tell some incredible stories!

Astral projection is a phenomenon – attracting increasing interest – which appears to have been experienced by both humans and animals.

Astral projection may occur when a loved one is thousands of miles away on the other side of the world, and through deep meditation and concentration, one is able to project one's consciousness to appear to the loved one. Animals pine for those they love and may project themselves to that person.

One such case concerns Michael, an eight-year-old boy who was torn away from his best friend, Shep, a German Shepherd dog, when his parents divorced. Michael emigrated with his mother to Australia and Shep stayed in England with Michael's father.

Prior to emigrating Michael had seen Shep almost every day. But now he had been wrenched far away and consequently fretted so much for his dog that it told on his health. He refused to eat and the asthma from which he had suffered since the age of three suddenly worsened. Michael became very ill and one evening he was rushed into hospital as a result of a bad asthma attack.

After extensive treatment Michael eventually settled down into a deep sleep and his exhausted mother fell asleep in a chair beside the bed. In the early hours of the morning she was awakened by Michael calling 'Shep! Shep!'

Michael was sitting up in bed, smiling broadly at something across the room. Looking in that direction his mother was amazed to see Shep sitting there staring over at Michael. However, when she jumped up and began to move towards Shep, the faithful dog slowly disappeared in front of their eyes.

Michael's mother was totally unable to believe what she had seen and she phoned her ex-husband in England, seeking confirmation that Shep was alright. She was told that he was fine, but had become very restless around the time that both she and Michael had seen him sitting in the hospital room in Australia.

The emotional bond between Michael and Shep was so profound that they had formed a telepathic link one with the other. When Michael was dangerously ill and rushed into hospital, Shep became aware of this, and his strong desire to be with Michael in time of crisis caused him to astrally project to Michael's bedside.

Not only are Newfoundland dogs extremely powerful creatures, possessing great physical strength, but they are also powerhouses of the healing force. These gentle giants of the canine world usually have lovely calm and friendly natures, and for this very reason they are very good dogs to have around children, the elderly and the infirm. This story concerns Demi, a three-year-old Newfoundland who was the constant companion of Mavis, a hard-working mother of three young children.

Mavis' husband David was a sea captain and, as he was away quite a lot, Demi was great company for Mavis. Needless to say, he was also a great favourite with the children, and helped to keep them entertained. He was a very affectionate creature, who loved to be cuddled and thrived on love and affection. In fact he was never happier than when he was the centre of attention which, of course, he very often was. To the children Demi was an animated teddy bear who was always ready for a game.

An elderly friend of the family, Gladys, had been ill for some time. She was recovering from her second stroke, but was now extremely depressed as a result of her ill health and had sunk so low that she would not talk to anyone. She would simply sit all day staring into space and would only take food when someone fed her. Knowing that Gladys was a dog lover, Mavis suddenly had the idea of taking Demi to see her, thinking that he would cheer her up.

Demi could be very persuasive and, as well as being the possessor of a wonderful personality, he was a real character, with a lovely sense of humour. Mavis was certain that he could help Gladys to get well.

Sure enough, just as Mavis had thought, within five minutes of trotting into her living room Demi had persuaded Gladys to stroke him, albeit in a half-hearted, absent-minded way to begin with. But 20 minutes later she was leaning forwards to cuddle him and before it was time for Mavis to leave Gladys was laughing at Demi's antics.

Mavis was thrilled at the change Demi had effected in Gladys in such a short time. Over the next few weeks she made an effort to take Demi to see Gladys as often as possible. As Mavis told me, Demi became Gladys' own P.A.T. dog, and he worked wonders.

Tom had not long been discharged from hospital when I met him, and he was still convalescing following a heart attack. His wife had died two years before and Felix – his beautiful tabby cat – was now the only family Tom had left. When I visited him at his home he told me that he found it extremely uncanny how his plump, three year old tabby knew exactly when he was feeling unwell.

Sensing how Tom felt, Felix would climb on to his lap and then stretch up, full length, and snuggle his head into the side of Tom's face and shoulder. There he would remain, purring contentedly until Tom felt better which, he assured me, was always very shortly after Felix's 'treatment'.

Olivia Freshgarden was in her mid-seventies. She had always been extremely healthy and had led an active energetic life until her husband Martin passed away. Although still physically healthy, Olivia started to suffer from panic attacks, which became so acute that she was eventually afraid to leave the safety of her home. She resigned herself to living the life of a recluse. The only person she would allow into her home was her daughter Alma and it was Alma who arrived one day with a rescue cat called Molly.

Molly was a four year old tortoiseshell feline who had been badly mistreated and was in great need of love. She took to Olivia immediately, and the feeling was mutual. Molly very quickly became aware of Olivia's anxiety neurosis, and whenever she felt that her owner was suffering, she would simply climb upon to her lap, as though in a friend's show of support.

Olivia soon realized that – along with the reassuring feeling of friendship – something special happened when Molly curled up on her lap. The panic attack, along with its accompanying feelings of complete terror and shortness of breath, abated within minutes. Molly also appeared to impart a wonderful feeling of calm and relaxation to Olivia. It was clear to her, she told me, that something other than moral support was exchanged when the warm, soft feline settled down on her lap. For Molly somehow discharged energy waves into Olivia, with the result that she felt peaceful, and felt all the physical symptoms of her fear slowly drain away.

It is now several years since Olivia last suffered a panic attack. She leads a normal, healthy life and is able to leave the 'safety' of her home. She even travelled overseas last year to visit her sister in Canada.

Babs, a seven-year-old Yorkshire Terrier, always looked forward eagerly to her regular nine o'clock walk with Pat and Frank, her two owners. Even after Frank died suddenly, at nine o'clock every evening Babs continued to place her lead expectantly on the arm of the chair where Frank had always sat. She would stand wagging her tail and staring eagerly, as if waiting for him to rise from his seat in front of the television.

The little dog could still see her master. Her actions gave a lot of comfort to Pat, who knew, through Bab's demeanour, that her husband was still around the home.

There are other stories in which the family dog has fretted so much following the death of its owner, that it simply gave up the will to live, and died seemingly of a broken heart. It would almost seem as though the little creature was overwhelmed with the desire to be with its master.

One of the most touching stories is of the little Skye Terrier, Greyfriar's Bobby, who was so devoted to its owner John Grey, that following John's death in 1858, Bobby remained beside his grave, refusing to move, wanting only to be close to his beloved master.

Bobby, as he was affectionately known by the townsfolk of Edinburgh, was 16 when he himself died in 1872, and he had been only two-years-old when John Grey died. So, for 14 years Bobby slept on his master's grave and only left it to visit those kindly folk who took it in turns to feed him.

This little dog was typical of one who had been shown a great deal of love and affection, which he reciprocated. He was loyal right up until the day he died.

Such stories transcend the bounds of coincidence; there are far too many of them and they bear striking similarities to one another. Of one thing though I am quite certain, and that is that animals are underestimated in every way and their loyalty extends much further than the loyalty of humans.

seven | Pet Astrology

Over the last 15 years or so a whole new concept of pet psychology has evolved. Many now believe that animals – just like humans – are influenced by the movements and positioning of the planets in the heavens. In the same way that our moods, emotions, and personalities differ according to the map of the heavens when we are born, animals too have different characteristics, likes and fears according to their star sign.

I am not suggesting that your cat or dog should check the astrology corner in the morning paper to see how their day is going to go. What I am suggesting is that a little study of your pet's psychic and astrological profile may enable you to understand it much more, and it will also help you to see exactly what lies behind the façade of the creature you think you know.

Let us take the example of Cancerians. The insecurities and sensitivity often seen in the true Cancerian human are also seen in the Cancerian cat or dog. The Cancerian person can be extremely emotional and very moody, but also quite communicative and very good with people. The cat or dog born under the sign of Cancer desperately needs and thrives on love and affection. It needs a secure and stable home life, and plenty of interactions with humans. It loves to be stroked and cuddled and without these things it very quickly develops emotional and sometimes psychological problems. More Cancerian people than we realize possess addictive personalities and often become slaves to anything that pleases the senses. The Cancerian cat or dog can be just the same and may quite easily develop an obsessive nature. More than all this though, the Cancerian creature often exhibits one of the strongest personalities, and usually possesses the most effective ability to heal. The more it is allowed to interact with the family, the more healing it is able to release into the home. In fact, the Cancerian pet is extremely family orientated and loves to be around people. Remember though, I am not talking about some nebulous feeling that effects us purely on a psychological level, but about a very potent force that has the power to effect healing in the human organism. Like humans, the creature born under the sign of Cancer is the most psychic of all animals – it is the most receptive and the strongest transmitter of the healing force.

This is not to say though that animals born under other astrological signs do not have such abilities. On the contrary, all animals, regardless of when they were born, have their own special psychic abilities. In my experience though, the 'water' signs – Cancer, Pisces and Scorpio do appear to be able to transmute and transmit the healing force in a more effective way.

Let us now turn our consideration to all 12 astrological signs and the way in which your pet is influenced and affected by them. Given this information you will then have a good idea of what exactly to look for in your pet, so that you can recognize and benefit from its particular qualities.

Aries Dog

Element Fire

This creature can be quite laid back, and although rather a sensitive animal and one which will always respond to love and affection, it can be quite stubborn, and will certainly not do anything it does not want to.

The dog born under the sign of Aries often appears to be lost in thought. However, this is not always the case, as the Aries dog knows exactly how to relax, and has somehow evolved the ability to simply 'turn off' the power, so to speak.

The dog born under the sign of Aries certainly likes comfort and once it has been allowed to curl up on the master's chair I am afraid that nothing will persuade it to move without taking umbrage. Yes, the dog born under the sign of Aries knows how to sulk.

The healing energies discharged by this dog are quite strong and very good for those humans who lack confidence and are over sensitive.

Aries Cat

This creature, unlike the dog, can be rather adventurous and is extremely nosy. It can be quite affectionate, but knows exactly when it has had enough. Although it is quite selective over the company it keeps, because of its likeable nature it is never without a collection of friends. This cat enjoys the comforts of home life, and although it likes to roam, it certainly knows when it is well off and so will always return home.

This cat's natural healing forces are extremely effective in aiding a distraught nervous system to normalize itself, and also to aid recovery after illness.

Taurus Dog

Element Earth

This creature possesses a healthy sense of fun and is perhaps one of the most practical of dogs. It likes pleasure and will go to any length to gratify its passions and desires.

The Taurus dog likes to over-indulge, and sometimes carries things to the extreme. If a dog can have a butterfly mind, then the Taurus dog has one. However, as with all Taurus personalities, this is a thoughtful, loving creature who is extremely faithful and very protective.

The dog born under the astrological sign of Taurus possesses extremely strong energies; just gently stroking its back will fill you with calmness and help to promote serenity and peace of mind. The energies that emanate from this creature will also bring relief to those painful arthritic limbs.

Taurus Cat

This creature can be extremely bossy, especially where humans are concerned, and is prone to sulking! Its jealous nature may prevent it from interacting well with other animals. However, the Taurus cat can also be quite sensual, and is extremely warm and affectionate.

This creature's healing energies tend to be very vibrant and have the effect of anaesthetizing the body to pain and anxiety. Its company is very calming on the mind and soul.

Gemini Dog

Element Air

The Gemini dog is full of character and knows exactly how to win hearts. Usually very kind by nature it quickly attunes itself to people's emotions. It is one of the most communicative of all astrological signs. His charismatic nature may win hearts but necessitates a side which can be unpredictably moody, nervous and even unstable.

However, meeting a Gemini dog often seems like meeting an old friend. It has a tail wag for anyone who bothers to say hello to it and will always offer a friendly paw to anyone who is feeling low. The Gemini dog possesses powerful, soothing healing abilities that are very effective where there is any sort of infection.

Gemini Cat

The Gemini cat possesses very sharp senses and is one of the most telepathic of creatures. It is usually very energetic with a strong sense of adventure. It has a cheeky mischievous side and the charisma to make everyone feel important.

Like the Gemini dog, the Gemini cat is extremely communicative and very loving. It possesses strong healing energies that are good for the treatment of almost any health condition.

Cancer Dog

Element Water

As I mentioned at the beginning of this chapter both the Cancerian dog and cat are the most psychic of all the astrological signs. But, there can be an extremely negative side to the Cancerian dog, which can become very depressed, the result of an inherent emotional nature.

The Cancerian dog is a very emotional creature and has a great deal of love to give. In fact, it lives to love and be loved. Love is life's sustenance to a Cancerian dog and is more important to it than the very air it breathes. It may not be the most energetic of dogs physically, but mentally it has been everywhere and done everything.

The Cancerian dog can heal you with love alone. Its energies are very strong and vibrant and somehow have an holistic effect upon the human organism.

Cancer Cat

Like the Cancerian dog, the Cancerian cat too is a dreamer, and one who is able to travel great distances in the vehicle of its mind – which is never still.

It too possesses strong and incredibly vibrant healing energies, which can have a pronounced positive effect upon the human mind. This cat is very good to have around children when they are feeling unwell.

Leo Dog

Element Fire

This creature possesses one of the strongest characters in the dog world and always likes to be the centre of attention. If dogs can be vain then the Leo dog most certainly is.

This canine is very strong and often exerts a great deal of power over its carers. He possesses the ability to influence the minds of its owners, and its energy can be extremely effective in the healing of headaches caused by tension, eyestrain or migraine. A cuddle from a Leo dog will relax you and take all your worries and pains away.

Leo Cat
Just like the Leo dog, the Leo cat likes to be made a fuss of, and may therefore find it difficult to accept other creatures – especially dogs – in the family home. It can be extremely impatient and often possesses a very volatile nature.

The Leo cat appears to have a soothing effect on the human mind, while at the same time an invigorating influence on the entire human organism. This creature will aid the healing process of any dermatological condition, and will give strength to the nervous system.

Virgo Dog

Element Earth
The investigative powers of this creature may sometimes be misconstrued as nosiness when, in fact, the Virgo dog simply likes to explore unknown territory and welcomes a challenge. This quality is demonstrated by its 'sniffer' characteristics; its nose probably being its most sensitive organ, and its sense of smell incredibly acute.

This is a fussy creature and may sometimes appear so snobby that it could almost have been born into the canine aristocracy. It likes its home comforts and pleasures.

Although possessing strong healing energies the Virgo dog can be quite miserable by nature, and it therefore has to feel happy and comfortable with someone before healing can take place. Nevertheless, its healing properties are effective when mobility of the limbs is restricted. It also aids recovery from illness by raising the levels of vitality in the human organism.

Virgo Cat

Like the Virgo dog, the Virgo cat has a sense of adventure and always welcomes a challenge. This is a very resilient creature who will take anything thrown at it (within reason, that is).

The Virgo cat likes to be stroked cuddled and bathed in affection. It is nearly always a creature of habit and is usually very tidy. It possesses a very strong and sharp memory and can quickly attune itself to a family atmosphere.

The Virgo cat's healing abilities extend over a wide area, and this cat is always good to have around when you are feeling unwell, or simply under the weather.

Libra Dog

Element Air

The dog born under the astrological sign of Libra is either very high or extremely low, in its emotional state; there is very rarely a happy medium. However, warm, friendly and extremely persuasive, this dog can overwhelm its owner with affection. This dog is the charmer of the canine world.

The Libra dog can release strong healing vibrations which are especially beneficial for sick and elderly people. It can calm an anxious person especialy when cuddled (which it loves to be). The only faults of the Libra dog is its volatile and unpredictable mood swings which may prevent it from releasing its full healing potential.

Libra Cat

This creature is full of personality and character. It possesses endless stores of energy and vitality and is extremely invigorating to have around the home.

The Libra cat is extremely wise and always prefers to take charge and control over other creatures in the home. This cat's healing abilities are extremely effective where psychological and emotional illnesses are concerned and will also help to ease intense physical pain.

Scorpio Dog

Element Water

The Scorpio dog is quiet and reserved with its feelings. It does not like to be cuddled too much and is a lover of its own company. This dog dislikes loud and boisterous people and due to its charismatic, yet understated charm, just being around a Scorpio dog can be healing in itself.

Its healing energies have the effect of strengthening and precipitating a sick person's own energies, and of helping to clear the mind. It can quite often be sufficient just to sit next to a Scorpio dog and stroke its fur gently a few times in order to receive its vibrant healing energies.

Scorpio Cat

The Scorpio cat possesses many of the qualities of the Scorpio dog: it is independent, quiet and occasionally standoffish. However, unlike the Scorpio dog, the cat simply cannot be still. It is forever on the move, both mentally and physically.

This creature's healing vibrations tend to have a very stabilizing effect upon the human mind, promoting serenity and calm within the nervous system. Its energies are quite cold and often feel like currents of electricity when one strokes its fur.

Sagittarius Dog

Element Fire

Although an extremely loveable character, this creature can often be difficult to control. Its energies are all over the place making him extremely inconsistent. It has so many things to do and very little time to do them in. It never seems to finish anything before it goes on to the next thing.

A spiritualized creature, the Sagittarius dog has a strong character and well-developed sense of humour. This dog gives a whole new meaning to animal individuality, and although it can be quite unpredictable, it can always be persuaded or encouraged with the use of the proverbial 'walkies'. Despite its irratic nature the Sagittarius dog is good to have around when one is feeling depressed or perhaps recovering from mental or emotional trauma.

Sagittarius Cat

This creature has a sense of fun and certainly knows how to enjoy life. In fact, not only does it appear to live life to the full, but there are not enough hours in a day for this feline to do all the things it wants to do. It loves to be loved and shown affecion and its fun nature tends to draw people and other animals towards it.

The cat born under the astrological sign of Sagittarius discharges its healing energies in consistent waves. These have a remarkable effect upon most illnesses, particularly in the elderly.

Capricorn Dog

Element Earth

This creature loves all the comforts of a secure and loving home life. Although a little laid back and stubborn, particularly in anxious moments, its fur never ruffles. This dog can be quite courageous and will often rush in where angels fear to tread.

These dogs are also extremely protective towards their owners, and do not welcome change at all. Moving home tends to make them feel somewhat moody and depressed, but being the resilient creatures they are, any negative emotions of self-pity and sadness are usually transient; the Capricorn dog will quickly return to its normal self. Its possessive and head strong nature can sometimes manifest as bossiness.

If dogs can be like 'old women' then the Capricorn dog is exactly that. Their natural instinct to mother their owners makes them magnificent healers and these dogs make wonderful P.A.T. dogs for the elderly or mentally disabled. They are usually fairly evenly tempered, they like to be pampered and made a fuss of, they give their energies selfishly to anyone who needs help.

Capricorn Cat

This creature possesses all the qualities of the Capricorn dog and more. It has an inherent need to care for all other creatures, and can sometimes be too clingy where its carer is concerned. This creature is good to have around in times of sickness, and it will certainly not stray too far from an owner who is unwell. The owner of a Capricorn cat will benefit greatly from its vibrant healing energies.

Aquarius Dog

Element Air

The dog born under the astrological sign of Aquarius nearly always possesses a pleasant and likeable disposition, and gives a whole new meaning to the saying 'Its bark is worst than its bite'. Although quite moody, it is a little pussycat really.

This creature appears to think a great deal, and has most certainly evolved a spiritual sensitivity. He is a natural healer, whose calming energies are effective on all manner of illnesses.

Aquarius Cat

This is one charismatic pussycat who can charm the birds out of the trees. Although not a malicious creature where birds are concerned, its playful nature can sometimes be misconstrued.

The cat born under the astrological sign of Aquarius will promote serenity and calmness in the human mind. Its warm fur will calm taut and anxious nerves.

Pisces Dog

Element Water

The Pisces dog can often appear cold and unapproachable, but in reality it is warm, loving and extremely friendly. Its cautious and sensitive nature can sometimes make it appear insecure, and although it can take offence occasionally, it dislikes very few people. This dog's sensitivity and insecurity necessitates an extremely loving home where it is treated as a part of the family.

This dog wants to heal everyone and make the whole world a better place to live in. Its healing powers are good for anyone suffering heart or respiratory conditions.

Pisces Cat

The Pisces cat is astute and perceptive. Its awareness is so sharp that you could almost cut yourself on its fur! Although affectionate in nature, it can be very cautious and will only allow you to invade its space when it is absolutely certain of your intentions.

Piscean energies are extremely effective in aiding the human organism to recover from illness. Its healing vibrations are very quick, and have the incredible effect of infusing a person with a surge of energy. This creature's fur is 'alive' with vitality, and just running one's fingers through it occasionally is indeed a tonic to the depleted and tired mind.

Although specific health conditions have been mentioned under each astrological sign, I feel it is important to point out that once the healing energy passes from your pet and is absorbed by your nervous system, the *whole* person receives healing treatment as opposed to merely the part that is affected.

eight | Mystical Dog

The mystical powers of dogs are becoming increasingly recognized. Their inspirational ability to work alongside humans and to interact with them so harmoniously, is a clear reflection of their wonderous qualities – qualities seen in no other animal. This chapter will be entirely devoted to exploring the special attributes of Man's Best Friend.

While I believe all dogs possess metaphysical healing powers to some greater or lesser degree, occasionally one comes across the *Mystical Dog* – a dog with exceptional intelligence and extraordinary powers. It may well be that such a dog lives with you in your home and you do not even know it. These dogs are the saints almost of the canine world and bring an awful lot of love into the family environment.

Dog who have unusually pleasant temperaments and dispositions psychically manifest a much softer energy field than the playful and boisterous creature whose energies appear to be all over the place. This creature's aura often appears quite pink, but when the dog is emotionally aroused – as is very much the case when it is stroked or cuddled by a person it loves – its energy field may become tinted with a delicate shade of blue. It is at this point that the dog may be seen to discharge fine subtle rays of different colours from its surrounding energy field. A psychic can witness these emanations as they infiltrate the human's aura, immediately affecting a subtle change in the aura's appearance.

When a person is stressed, or perhaps feeling a little under the weather, interaction with a Mystical Dog will have an immediate calming effect. The dog's powers will also precipitate a spontaneous increase of vitality in the person's whole body.

A dog's metabolism is extremely fast, this results in the dog burning up far greater amounts of personal vitality than most other creatures. With so much energy being let out, a dog must be able to draw in great streams of power; this can be quite astounding. Yogic masters often demonstrate such abilities when practising specifically designed breathing techniques, thus controlling the in-flowing force of vitality. This practice of controlled breathing enables them to exercise greater control over their bodies, and thus cultivates stronger mental or psychic powers; in yoga they are termed 'Siddhis.'

Many farm dogs, particularly those who work with sheep, possess great stores of universal vitality in their bodies. These creatures are extremely therapeutic to have around when one is feeling low in vitality, as is the case when recovering from illness or surgery.

The farm canine possesses a specific kind of aura, exhibiting delicate shades of eggshell or coral pink. They constantly emit streams of vitality into the surrounding environment, and are always extremely effective in the healing of psychological or emotional conditions. Because of their high vitality levels, farm dogs do not like to be held in confined spaces as this restricts their vitality output.

Long-haired dogs, in most cases, have a more calming effect on human metabolism than short-haired breeds. They tend to control the in-flowing vitality a little more efficiently than short-haired breeds. Creatures with short, wiry hair appear to have a gift for healing aching arthritic limbs, and can also be effective upon conditions causing depression.

The extremely good-natured dog with a quiet well-behaved manner often stands out amongst the more boisterous, inquisitive personalities of the canine world. This dog is usually highly observant and quietly passes on its healing energies to any one who happens to need them. These quiet, mystical dogs are often very wise, extremely good with children, careful around the sick, elderly or disabled, and unusually good with their paws. This dog is not greedy where food is concerned, and in fact sees food only as a necessity to sustain it. It very often enjoys the same food as the rest of the family.

Although many may believe that dogs do not possess the same kind of intelligence as man, the Mystical Dog most certainly exhibits evidence of an advanced intelligence. In fact these dogs can seemingly do all but talk, and even this they attempt to achieve.

This dog is very much a dreamer, and may often lie in front of the fire just staring into the glowing flames, but at all times with ears pricked as its psychic radar continually scans the surrounding atmosphere ready for action. Its senses are very sharp and always acutely attuned to its surroundings. Nothing will pass this mentally busy creature unnoticed. It is always 'turned on and tuned in' and although it nearly always derives a great deal of benefit from its slumber, it is often an extremely light sleeper and will awaken at the slightest sound.

Although it might appear to be a very serious dog, the Mystical Dog possesses an incredible sense of humour, and even the more mature furry creature is blessed with puppy-like vitality.

From an early age the Mystical Dog will be behaved and house-trained without any formal training; it will sit at the door until it is opened to allow it to answer a call of nature. In fact a dog of this kind will demonstrate many things without any training. My Old English Sheepdog, Harry, was a classic example of such a creature. From the very tender age of three months, every so often he would simply sit down, tilt his head to one side, and raise a paw straight up, high above his head. We quickly learned that he did this when he wanted someone to give him a cuddle – and believe me, a cuddle from an Old English Sheepdog is the cuddle of all cuddles. This was also Harry's way of imparting his extremely powerful healing. Although quite a large dog, his healing vibrations were quite gentle and very calming.

Harry appeared to carry a lot of vitality in his ears, as well as in his paws. Simply passing his ear through my fingertips, over and over, was an incredible tonic, which I personally found very relaxing after a stressful day.

Harry, though, was an unusual dog, and one who never really knew good health himself. He was a huge presence in my home, and both physically and spiritually filled every corner of it with warmth and love. I have no doubt that Harry was a truly Mystical Dog.

So, to reiterate, when speaking about the healing powers of animals I am most definitely not just speaking about the comfort and warmth we experience when cuddling or stroking our dogs. I am in fact referring to a metaphysical transference of energy; energy that is found in all living organisms, but which is predominant in animals, particularly in cats and dogs.

Where does this healing force come from? Many believe that this force comes to us primarily from the sun, as well as through the food we eat and the water we drink. I personally argue that it is in stored in the solar plexus from where it is distributed throughout the physical body to the various organs where it is needed.

Whilst humans somehow have difficulty in retaining this powerful energy, animals do not. In fact, the animal organism is able to store huge amounts of this vitality, and it is because of this that they are able to emanate extremely effective healing vibrations.

However, some humans are able to retain this energy quite naturally. Although these people are in the minority, they do appear to have extremely strong healing powers. I am quite certain that most people have had the experience of being in the presence of someone who has the ability to make us feel invigorated, especially when we are feeling a little down or perhaps under the weather. It is not so much what this person says or does, as it is simply being in their presence. They have an uplifting effect on all around them and often draw many strangers into their presence. Animals have exactly the same effect, only their release of vitality is far more specific and can have a holistic effect upon the person. Because animals are able to draw in such great amounts of this energy quite naturally from the air, they are like powerful generators which we humans can learn to connect to.

Pets can save lives, and they most definitely restore sanity.

nine | Meditating With Your Pet

Are you aware that you can attune your mind to your pet and communicate with it? I am quite certain that most people will dismiss this suggestion as being quite ridiculous. The truth is though, the closer the relationship you have with your pet, the stronger and more profound your communications will be.

There are so many things about your pet's true character that you do not see. Most people tend to take their pets for granted, and often wrongly assume – simply because they use a completely different system of communication – that their cat or dog cannot 'speak'. The frequency of an animal's mind is much higher than ours and, being unencumbered by those things that cause us so much stress and anxiety, there is far greater clarity in the reception and transmission of their thought processes. So through careful attunement to your pet's vibrations you can learn to talk to it, and with practice you may in fact become quite proficient at understanding exactly how it is feeling and what it is trying to say to you.

By the shifting of your consciousness in meditation, until the correct frequency has been acquired, you will be able to understand that universal language of thought, enabling you to then break down the subtle barrier that separates the human mind from that of the animal's. There is certainly nothing complicated in the process. All you need to do to meditate with your pet is to pick the right moment. This will be when both you and your pet are quiet and relaxed.

PET MEDITATION – STAGE I

- Sit comfortably beside your pet, either on the floor or on the sofa.
- With your eyes closed simply stroke your pet gently, feeling the warmth of its fur between your fingertips.
- At the same time mentally reassure it of your love for it.
- Feel a deep spiritual bond with your pet, and be conscious of its love and devotion for you.
- Become totally relaxed, allowing your breathing to be nice and rhythmical, slow and deep.
- Now, in your mind's eye, see your pet leading you through an archway of intense golden light. Follow it, and emerge into a spacious hall with a glass-domed ceiling.
- Look up at the glass dome, and see that it is translucent, like mother-of-pearl.
- Around you the walls of the hall appear to shimmer with many different colours and there is a sweet fragrance in the air.
- Bright light cascades down from the domed ceiling, breaking up into a myriad of colours as it falls into the centre of the hall, forming a pool of sparkling light there.

- Follow your pet to this point in the centre of the hall and allow yourself to be bathed in the different colours.
- Feel that closeness and oneness with your pet, and feel as though you are floating on a coloured cloud. Try to become even more relaxed.
- Now allow yourself to move mentally across the spacious hall towards the far side.
- Having reached the wall see yourself passing through it, as if by magic, and find yourself and your pet back in your living room, both feeling totally relaxed and at peace.

This exercise in visualization must be repeated several times, at least once a day, if practical, over a period of some weeks, before moving on to the next phase of meditation. Once you feel quite comfortable with the exercise, and have no problems at all creating the imagery, you may consider the following phase:

PET MEDITATION – STAGE 2

- Sit quietly next to your pet.
- Close your eyes and place one hand gently on its head.
- Stroke its head and neck slowly, with your fingertips. When you feel as though 'something' is passing from you to your pet, establish this extremely important connection by sending some simple mental commands to it, such as 'If you can hear me, stretch your body,' or perhaps 'Lick my hand'.

- At first there may be no positive response from your pet as it may simply not be listening to you. Some animals have an extremely short attention span, so this phase of the experiment might take quite a lot of patience on your part.
- It may be, though, that your pet responds immediately. This will depend on whether or not your furry creature is in 'receive mode'.
- Once you have received a response a further mental command must be given – one which requires some physical effort from your pet.
- Try 'Go to your bowl and have a drink of water' for example. Send this command no more than three times.
- Should there still be no response, leave it for a short while before trying again.
- Take time with the experiment, and even if it takes weeks or months try to persevere with it. If you have a good relationship with your pet it will work.
- It may also be a good idea to keep a record of your results, so that you can make a study of them. This may perhaps help you to see which approach would be the best and most effective.

When you are absolutely certain that the results achieved represent your pet's positive responses to your mental commands, the next step is to listen to what it is saying to you.

It is thought that before even the most rudimentary form of speech was evolved primitive man communicated his thoughts and feelings telepathically. Working on the premise that this process of thought transference is possible, it should also apply to the thoughts of animals.

As one would imagine the thinking process of an animal is completely different to ours. I doubt very much that they mentally contemplate the mysteries of the universe, or even try to work out some complicated mathematical equation. However, one can rest assured that animals certainly do *think*. The minds of both cats and dogs are very much like radar, and are often continually scanning their surroundings. Animals also possess the ability to recall events that have been significant or important in some way to them – and not only simple instructions which have been repeated several times.

Once a dog or cat forms a deep emotional tie with a human, that person becomes the main focus of the creature's life. Although dogs demonstrate this emotional attachment more than cats, a cat still allows a deep bond to be formed with its human owner.

PET MEDITATION – STAGE 3

Once a meditative rapport has been created with your pet, and the previous experimental processes have been practiced regularly – and with some degree of success – spend some time relaxing with your pet in a nice quiet spot.

- It is often said that cats and dogs think in pictures. However, these transmitted pictures are sometimes converted automatically into definite thoughts.
- Speak to your pet mentally, making quite sure that you speak very slowly. Although the thought processes of animals are of a much higher frequency than those transmitted by the human mind, when an animal is receiving our thoughts it needs time to focus and to comprehend.

- So, when you transmit a question to your pet, do it several times and then pause for a minute.
- Alternatively, convert your question as well as you can into pictures or easy to understand symbols. You may need time to consider exactly how you are going to do this.
- When you have decided which pictures you are going to use, ensure that you have condensed the question into as few pictures as possible, and then transmit them to your pet in a rhythmical and consistent way.
- Although animals are far from stupid, their attention span can be quite short and sometimes extremely limited. So, if you are asking your dog to go and retrieve something from the next room, one of its toys for example, make every effort to create one picture as opposed to a sequence of pictures to represent the question. Neither cats nor dogs can cope with complicated questions and nor do they enjoy making decisions.
- A simple question such as 'Are you happy?' should receive an immediate response. Always include your pet's name at the end of the question, for example 'Are you happy, George?'
- With a question such as this transmitting your feelings will suffice, as opposed to pictures. The most common response to this question is often more a physical one, such as a lick, a paw, a wag, rather than a thought.

Just spending time close to your pet, enjoying its wonderful healing vibrations, and listening to the vibratory motion of its body, will enable you very quickly to become attuned to its mind, and to understand the language it is speaking. Developing this ability to speak to your pet also enables you to know when it is unwell, or feeling sad for some reason. Once it realizes that you are making an effort to communicate with it, your pet will endeavour to help you all it can.

Another interesting point is that animals are either attracted to, or repelled by, certain colours. You may notice, for instance, that your cat likes to curl up on the table when there is a blue tablecloth draped over it. Or perhaps it enjoys sleeping on the chair with pink covers, or by the window with yellow glass.

If you have noticed your pet's preferences for certain colours, it might just be more sensitive to colour vibrations than you think. Should this be the case I would suggest that you teach it the names of the different colours, so that you can use these as vehicles for your communications.

In your experiments you may like to place differently coloured cushions around the room. When you know for certain that your pet is responding to your questions, ask it to go to the blue cushion, then to the yellow cushion, then the pink one, and so on. You may think that this is perhaps taking it all a little too far, but experimentation should quickly dispel this notion.

People who work seriously with animals, and who are dedicated to their work – vets, or those who work in animal shelters – often, without even realizing it, become so attuned to animals that they know exactly what they are thinking or even how they are feeling.

It is not as difficult to understand the language of animals as one might imagine. If you have a close relationship with your pet you are halfway to understanding what exactly your pet is saying to you. Look upon it as merely speaking a different language, but one that you can most certainly learn.

ten | Man's Cruelty to the Animal Kingdom

We most certainly need animals far more than we know. Few of us recognize the pivotal role animals play in the evolution of man's emotions. In fact, their very presence on this planet alone creates a healing atmosphere that is vitally important to the spiritual equilibrium of humanity.

The dawn chorus and the movement of wings against the air are integrated parts of some mystical symphony composed by nature, which is so essential for the continuity of life. We should therefore feel privileged to share this planet with the Animal Kingdom, and it is time to realize that our need for them is far greater than we are presently able to understand.

However, there are some people in this world who are not just content to dislike animals, but they actually delight in subjecting them to the most appalling cruelty, without experiencing a hint of shame, guilt or conscience. These individuals often look upon animals as creatures without souls, or simple disease carriers possessing no feelings or awareness.

Cruelty to animals is by no means restricted to cats and dogs. On the contrary, the whole of the Animal Kingdom is affected in one way or another, from the cruel hunting of the fox, to the senseless slaughter of the noble elephant in Africa for their ivory tusks.

In recent years we have seen the horrific torture of the bear in China. Kept alive in the most hideous conditions its bile is extracted regularly and painfully from its gut, simply to provide a so-called 'miracle cure' – mainly for consumption in the Western world.

Whilst most people could not withstand either the stench and horror of an abattoir, or the sight of those defenceless and terrified creatures being led to their slaughter, those same people can, however, tuck into a succulent steak, or tear the flesh from a breast of chicken. The fact that they are eating the corpse of a living creature is nearly always conveniently ignored.

Humans are conditioned from childhood to believe that eating the flesh of animals is acceptable. To salve our consciences further we refer to the Bible, in which we can read how the flesh of the fatted calf was consumed. Eating meat must be alright then, we tell ourselves, as it is mentioned in the Bible. Anyway, as long as someone else does the slaughtering, and we do not have to see any blood flowing, or hear any screams of terror, or see any heaps of still, warm corpses, then consuming the cooked product on our plates is fine.

After all, why should meat-eating be any more acceptable than consuming human flesh? For animals are animated by the same force that animates the human form, and they are in fact a lot closer to God, and far more reliable than we humans.

Although meat-eating has always been a part of our culture, at least in the Western world, attitudes are certainly now beginning to change towards the habit. Science informs us that meat in our diet is no longer vitally important for a healthy body.

Dogs, rats, mice, monkeys and many more defenceless animals are being subjected to laboratory experiments in the name of science; do the creatures themselves possess a voice that protests? Or is their wellbeing reliant on those dedicated and courageous people who speak for them, and continually proclaim that 'Animals do have rights'?

Yes: there is most certainly a voice that speaks, and this voice is collectively made up of every single animal on this planet, creating a force which is far greater and more powerful than any exhibited by man.

Each and every animal on this planet is linked one to the other, in a mystical network within which a powerful force is created and passed around. Even the family dog, secure in the love of the family, is not ignorant of the plight and torment of its brother animals in far off places, for he too is an integral part of this great animal network.

But what of those who inflict so much misery and suffering on animals, and whose cruel acts often evade the punishment of the law? Is justice ever brought about?

By inflicting suffering of any kind upon an innocent creature, one might as well inflict suffering upon oneself. The Animal Kingdom as a whole is the very foundation upon which the evolution of man's emotional nature has its true being.

Cruelty to animals never passes unrecognized as the perpetrators of such cruelty take upon themselves great spiritual burdens. Consequently, the pain they inflict upon an innocent creature is eventually returned to them two-fold, if not in this life, then most certainly in the next.

But apart from man's wilful malice towards animals, we should not forget the thoughtless and careless destruction of animals in our countryside and on our roads. The wild bird population is decreasing enormously in numbers as more and more birds are seen lying dead on country roads. Unaware of the danger, millions of hedgehogs are dying beneath the wheels of cars because of man's haste and lack of care. The fox is hunted down by packs of specially trained dogs, while man looks on in delight. Badgers are baited, rabbits are either shot or killed on the roads, pheasants and grouse are allowed to grow fat until the season when they can 'lawfully' be shot.

Cruelty to animals varies from culture to culture, and surely represents the degree of spirituality attained therein. A great deal of cruelty exhibited towards the Animal Kingdom appears to have 'entertainment' value, which makes it more acceptable to the people of that particular country. Bull fighting is a prime example – a hideous and extremely cruel 'sport' in which no mercy is shown to that magnificent creature, which is tormented and tortured until it is finally killed.

In the same country donkeys are thrown from the tops of buildings during certain festive occasions. If the creature is lucky it will die immediately, if not it will suffer a slow, agonizing death. It has been said that it is only the uneducated of the country that participate in such barbaric events. I am quite certain that this is no excuse!

It would appear that because animals cannot speak with words that we understand, they are often regarded as mindless, soul-less creatures, without feelings, hopes or dreams.

The entire Animal Kingdom is being exploited, and is slowly diminishing in size, but still these innocent creatures continue to provide us with so much enjoyment. Their very presence on this planet creates a subtle atmosphere of healing, which permeates the very air we breathe and touches the very core of our being. *We simply could not live on a planet devoid of animals,* for, along with the food we eat, the water we drink, and the air we breathe, animals are indeed an essential part of human life.

But today a new epoch is beginning to dawn, as a wave of compassion, understanding and respect for nature and the

Animal Kingdom passes through man's collective conscious-ness. Although this 'new' awareness will pass by, sadly unheeded by the majority of our planet's human residents, that minority whose consciousness has already, or is now in the process of unfolding, will find themselves moving closer to a spiritual awakening.

Throughout the ages many great writers, philosophers and orators have put into words their own deepest feelings regarding animals and man's treatment of them. I have listed some of their quotations here, many of which I am sure you will find moving, as I do:

Animals share with us the privilege of having a soul.

PYTHAGORAS BC551

On seeing a dog being beaten, pitying he said 'Stop and beat it not, for the soul is that of a friend'.

XENOPHANES BC545

What have the oxen done, these faithful guileless beasts, harmless and simple, born to a life of toil?

OVID BC43

Hurt not animals.

TRIPTOLEMUS AD 50

A righteous man regardeth the life of his beast.

OLD TESTAMENT PROVERBS XII, 10

No beast is there on earth or fowl that flieth, nothing have we passed over in the book of Eternal Decrees, that shall not be gathered unto the Lord.

KORAN

There is not an animal on the earth, nor a flying creature on two wings, but they are people like unto you.

KORAN

A fleet horse or greyhound does not make a noise when they have done well ... Neither should man.

MARCUS AURELIUS

Animals have rights in themselves because of their capacity to feel both pain and pleasure.

St CIARAN OF OSSORY

God created humans and animals for their mutual benefit.

St COLMEILLE OF IONA

The pious duty of children is to feed their parents, and dogs and horses must also receive their food.

CONFUCIUS

All things are born of the unborn, and from this unity of life flows brotherhood and compassion for all creatures.

BUDDHA

In Buddhism we are told that animals possessed of the Buddha nature are in time destined for heaven.

CHRISTMAS HUMPRYES

The great lovers of men have also been great lovers of animals. St Francis of Assisi and his wolf; St Hugh of Lincoln and his swan; St Jerome and his lion; St Peter and the cock; St Benedict and the raven; St John the Evangelist and his red-legged partridge.

Revd. W.H. BARNARD

The behaviour of men to the lower animals, and their behaviour to each other, bear a constant relationship.

HERBERT SPENCER

Men who have practised tortures on animals without pity, relating them without shame. How can they still hold their heads high among human beings?

Dr SAMUEL JOHNSON

Thou wast not born for death, immortal bird!

JOHN KEATS

God made all creatures, and gave them our love and our fear,
To give sign, we and they are his children, one family here.

ROBERT BROWNING

The animal world is a manifestation of God's power, and demands respect and consideration. The desire to kill animals, unnecessary harshness and callous cruelty towards them, must always be condemned.

POPE PIUS XII

The love of an animal is in their eyes.

PHINEAS FLETCHER

... Medicine with cruel heartlessness has tortured sensitive animals in reckless scientific investigation with no direct or indirect relation to human good.

BISHOP PHILLIPS BROOKS

The greatness of a nation and their moral progress can be judged by the way their animals are treated.

GANDHI

If we have spirits that persist, the animals have; if we know after death who we are, they do.

JOHN GALSWORTHY

In studying the traits and dispositions of the so-called lower animals, and contrasting them with man's, I find the result humiliating to me.

MARK TWAIN

Vivisection brings a tremendous amount of suffering on the animal kingdom, which man has no right to inflict upon them.

Air Chief Marshall LORD DOWDING

We have a special duty to all animals, and we must fight against the merchants of animal suffering who subordinate compassion to the heartless demands of so-called scientific progress.

EDGAR LUSTGARTEN

Wild animals never kill for sport. Man is the only one to whom the torture and death of his fellow creatures is amusing in itself.

J.A.FROYDE

One of the best ways to reduce animal suffering is to convince scientists that animals are not necessary for medical research, and that alternative methods exist.

COLIN SMITH

Do not caress an animal with one hand and pick its bones with another.

TALL PINE

The sad and most disappointing thing to me is that those who dislike and are cruel to animals would not even think of reading this book.

eleven | The Wrong Programme

For humans the possibility that we survive bodily death has always held a great fascination. The very idea that we might be given the opportunity to be reborn once again into the physical world, for a continued corporeal existence, is even more exciting.

Although the concept of rebirth does not appear in modern day Christian philosophy it did form an integral part of early Christian teachings. Christianity though is quite specific about its ideas of the survival of the human soul, and these ideas exclude animals completely, even though the Animal Kingdom has played such an important role in the work of numerous saints throughout the ages. The Church has always cloaked the after-death experience in mystery, and made any knowledge of it accessible only through its priests and ministers.

As animals have always been looked upon as the lesser, although innocent creatures in the scheme of things, the chance of them being re-born into another corporeal life, let alone surviving the physical death, seems to many people unthinkable. To complicate the whole issue even more, the concept of rebirth is not as straight forward as one might imagine, or at least not where animals are concerned.

Whereas many believe that humans make a definite and clear choice about subjecting themselves to re-embodiment, animals do not have that choice. They are therefore drawn into the great wheel of rebirth in accordance with their evolutionary status, and from a profound need to pull themselves away from the endless cycle of rebirth.

However, the incredible intelligence of some domestic animals makes it quite apparent that there is something other than animal instinct in operation, and that some creatures are most certainly nearing the end of their great journey of perpetual rebirth.

Although I have already addressed the concept of reincarnation in chapter five, here I shall discuss the actual *Programming* of each life.

As with humans, animals too are born into a particular programme. The human soul has a specific mission when it is incarnated into a physical body, and has to fulfil certain spiritual needs. Eradicating habits, and developing those qualities that are absent, certainly do form an integral part of this mission, but for the animal soul the Great Cycle of Rebirth is a necessity and cannot be avoided.

Through this process the animal develops tolerance, sensitivity and an understanding of man. The lives of some animals often appear to be no more than a punishment for them, and yet this life often produces animals with the gentlest of natures.

Looking into the eyes of some animals one often sees a wise creature staring out as though saying 'What am I doing here in this body? Please help me. I should not be here.'

For some reason during the great mysterious process of rebirth, things can go wrong as the soul begins its vibratory descent. Its attainments and previous life memories maybe allowed to filter through into the creature's consciousness, when in fact all this data should be stored, and inaccessible to the incarnated soul. This causes the animal to be extremely sensitive, and to be in the possession of an almost human-like intelligence. These creatures possess a deep understanding of humans, and nearly always exhibit qualities that set them apart from other animals.

A whole group of animals can find themselves caught up in 'The Wrong Programme' when the process of reincarnation takes place. When affected collectively the individual animals may experience extremely difficult and at worst unhappy lives. They may be born into an environment of cruelty and deprivation, and be subjected to the most difficult and sad existence.

Because the pitiful creature has been so unfortunate as to incarnate through the wrong programme, its life is but a short sojourn in comparison to what might have been had the process gone according to plan. Such unfortunate creatures experience a brief rest after death, before then being drawn back into the Great Wheel of Rebirth.

On their return to the physical world they prove to be a huge presence, possessing an incredible intelligence and persona. Such animals possess amazing psychic abilities, and their very presence in a family creates a wonderful healing balm that cannot fail to affect all who come into contact with it.

Although these sorts of family pets are often extremely difficult to define, when in their presence one often has the strong feelings of standing before a creature greater than the average domesticated pet. They very often appear extremely wise and exude personality and character. This furry creature enjoys human company and loves to be touched. It interacts perfectly well with humans, takes extreme care with children and disabled people, and knows exactly when its owner is unhappy or unwell. They very quickly establish themselves as the 'head' of the household and the most important member in the family. In fact, these little creatures are not only huge characters with magnificent senses of humour, but their charm also enables them to win over the coldest of hearts.

In my quest for material for this book I learned of a man who had spent most of his adult life in and out of prison for committing crimes of violence. He was a persistent offender whose life was in chaos. He was lonely and very unhappy, causing him to drink more than he should, and this over-indulgence only contributed even more to his aggression and violence.

Life for Kenny changed dramatically when he rescued a young mongrel that was being savaged by two Alsations in the park. Both Kenny and Little Totty (as Kenny named the dog) escaped with only a few cuts and bruises, but Kenny's heart had been won almost immediately.

This special tiny mongrel and he became very close friends. Within weeks Kenny's drinking had practically stopped. He became more relaxed and much more pleasant to be around. Little Totty seemed to take all the aggression and anger away from him, and Kenny suddenly developed a completely different attitude towards everything and everyone. There was no doubt about it – Kenny became a different person altogether.

This all happened in 1993. Kenny is now in regular employment, and has not been in trouble with the police since Totty came into his life. In fact, he is now making plans to marry his girlfriend of two years. The credit for all this goes to Little Totty. Kenny proudly tells anyone who will listen to him that the dog has healed and transformed his life completely.

I recall as a child a stray dog running into our house on a cold foggy January night. Jack, as we affectionately called him, stayed with us as our guest for three years, winning his cheeky way into all our hearts.

Being myself a somewhat sickly child, often at home ill, Jack became my constant companion and friend. He slept beside me, played with me and protected me.

Then, one similar cold, foggy night, as though he was called away by some sacred mysterious voice, Jack ran off, never to be seen again. He took with him a huge piece of our hearts. Jack had most certainly been born on the wrong programme, and frequently appeared to be lost in thought, his large brown eyes always anxiously searching around him.

A family near to where I used to live in Liverpool, had a very affectionate and extremely cheeky wire-haired terrier. Everyone in the neighbourhood knew Winnie – short for Winston – and adored him.

Although we already had a dog (at that time it was Lucky) Winnie used to call to our house, literally knocking on the door, to come in and sit by the fire for a short while. My mother would give him a bowl of hot tea and something to eat, and then he would quietly leave, pausing for a moment on the step to look back and say 'Thank you' with a wag of his tail. We always felt privileged having Winnie visit us almost daily for five years.

Suddenly though his visits stopped. No one had seen any-thing of him. Then one day an envelope dropped through the letterbox. It contained a 'Thank you' card from Winnie's own-ers. It read: 'Thank you for showing so much kindness to Win-nie our much loved dog, who died of pneumonia last week.'

The strange thing was that while we knew that Winnie did have a good home, and that he was known to everyone in the neighbourhood, we actually believed that we were, in fact, the only family that Winnie visited. How wrong we were. Everyone in the street received the same 'Thank you' card for showing such kindness to a much-loved dog. In fact, everyone in the street had been hospitable to Winnie at one time or another, and he had obviously made it his business to visit everyone in turn.

Winnie had definitely been born into the wrong programme. He had a certain kind of wisdom, and always looked as though he was a soul who just did not belong in the body of a dog. He most certainly understood nearly every word that was said to him and could reply with a 'woof' or a paw. Winnie was also a great source of comfort to many of the elderly in the neighbourhood who used to look forward to his visits. Winnie was certainly a very old soul.

twelve | Cross My Paw With Silver

Dogs and cats are far more in tune with the future than we humans. We spend much of our time reminiscing about the past and remembering 'the good old times'; we are used to looking back as opposed to looking forward.

Time, it would seem, is a mystery to man. Our ephemeral minds somehow have great difficulty in comprehending the true concept – that time is the greatest of all illusions. In fact, the only way in which man can actually understand time is by compartmentalizing the events of his life into a Past, Present and Future.

Animals do not have this problem, for they do not have any real experiences or events to relate to. They appear to be much more relaxed about time, living perpetually in one eternal *now*. They seem to be able to glimpse the future at any time they want to, and what exactly they perceive of their future is already present to them in their *now*.

The Animal Kingdom appears to have no problem at all dipping mentally into the great vortex of time, where the Past, Present and Future manifest as *one*.

This ability is in fact the fundamental principle that underlies and controls the gift possessed by mystics and many psychics. Animals though have always possessed this ability, and it is partly this that enables them to sense danger when it is still far away and which also allows the dog or cat to know exactly when its owner is on the way home.

If dogs or cats were able to speak our language, or perhaps if we could learn to speak theirs, we would realize that, in theory, they possess the ability to foretell our future. In fact, the very thought of walking into a fairground fortune teller's booth, to be greeted by an Old English Sheepdog or perhaps a Labrador sitting quietly gazing into a crystal ball, waiting to tell our fortune, is certainly not as ridiculous as it sounds. I am quite sure that our pets are already looking into our futures, although what they see there they wisely keep to themselves.

Let us suppose that these powers could be exploited by us, and that having learned to communicate with them, our pets were then able to advise us of emotional, business and even health matters pertaining to our future.

It seems to be fairly easy to train our dogs to do specific tasks, so why not train them to use their psychic powers to our advantage? Your Spaniel might tell you to sell the car now before the mechanical problems start in two months time. Your Labrador might advise you on future business transactions, or your Afghan Hound might tell you to get a health checkup, or not to take a holiday to a particular country next month.

You may smile, but this, I am quite certain, is what will happen in the future. The more animals are encouraged to interact with humans, the more they will evolve a sensitivity towards us, and the ability to communicate with us.

In fact, a dog talking is not as ridiculous as it sounds. Some species of dogs appear to be so intelligent that it is quite clear that their evolutionary processes will eventually develop in them communicative faculties that will enable them to speak.

Although most dog and cat lovers talk to their pets, in the future our pets will be able to talk back and hold long conversations with us and we with them. In fact, the possibilities are endless. Imagine your dog or cat telling you exactly what kind of day it has had, and asking you what your day has been like. This surely must happen, considering the way in which a lot of domestic animals are evolving. Imagine your dog having an argument with you because it did not want to be placed in kennels while you went on your annual holiday, or perhaps disagreeing with you about your intense dislike of the dog next door. Imagine your dog shouting at you, 'How many times have I told you not to buy that brand of dog food?'

Dogs are already halfway to being little people. Were they to develop the ability to speak, I am quite sure they would have a lot to say. Imagine what it would be like in the future if dogs were able to speak for themselves. What a different world then it would be if our pets could only speak.

But I am quite certain that they would tell us what they know of our future, and would put their psychic abilities to good use, perhaps to help mankind, and to restore peace on the planet. But then, why should they when we have been so cruel to the Animal Kingdom?

Some dogs have only a superficial control over their psychic abilities, whilst others are able to use them all the time. This difference in ability I believe depends largely upon your dog's temperament, and is greatly influenced by the astrological sign it was born under. Some signs are most certainly more receptive than others, as shown in chapter seven on Pet Astrology.

As with people some dogs are thinkers, whilst others appear to have butterfly minds and have great difficulty in concentrating on anything at all for very long. The thinking dog is usually the most psychic. This creature needs a great deal of stimulation and appreciates its master speaking to it whenever possible. It also loves music. It is a very intelligent dog, and possesses a great capacity to learn, and to learn very quickly. Also, watch how its gaze often moves around a room, as though seeing something you cannot.

The canine and feline worlds are certainly much more in tune with the more subtle areas of the universe than we are, and they can therefore see, hear and sense far more than we can. A dog or cat is nearly always the first to sense an unpleasant atmosphere, even when we are totally oblivious to it. They are also able to sense anger and evil, fear and anxiety, and are always fully aware of those who do not like them, and just as aware of those who do.

Take a look at a dog who is loved and cared for, as opposed to the one who is not. Love encourages a dog to almost shine, not just psychically, but in everyway possible. The eyes of an unloved dog are dull and almost cry out for love. Its aura is dull, and it emits such a strong sense of sadness, that anyone with a degree of sensitivity could not fail to feel it.

Animals ask for nothing other than to be loved. They know full well that is exactly why they are here on this planet – to love and to be loved. Maybe the future will see an animal revolution, and perhaps then we will have to pay our pets for their services. Then, I am quite sure they will say, 'Cross my palm with silver'.

thirteen | Colour Power and Your Pet

As I have already mentioned dogs and cats are extremely sensitive to colour, and surrounding it with specific shades and tones of colour can often calm down a boisterous creature. However, much more than this can be achieved by combining the powerful energies of colour with your pet's own healing forces.

Living in a house with a psychically unpleasant atmosphere will not only create a lot of unhappiness and depression in the occupants, but at worst it can cause the health of the family to deteriorate, and may also plunge the household into the mire of misfortune. An unlucky house may not have anything to do with the present occupants, but may be the result of a build up of negative psychic energy brought about by the emotions and attitudes of all those who have lived there previously.

A house that is charged with negative psychic energy is often like a time bomb ready to go off, or even like a volcano on the point of eruption. The more unpleasant feelings it creates, the more powerful it becomes, as the minds of its occupants perpetuate this energy even more with further feelings of despondency, sadness and depression. And so it goes on.

It matters very little how long the family have lived in the house, and they may have always been unhappy there, but the time bomb can explode at any moment, or the volcano erupt, precipitating the dormant negative energies into action.

The thoughts, feelings and emotions emanating from the minds of the occupants of a house, upon being evolved, impregnate the psychic structure of the house itself, infusing it with power and vitality. So, gradually the house becomes alive with a living personality all of its own. The subtle character that has been created in the house in fact represents all the minds of the people who have lived there throughout the years. It becomes a sort of paranormal schizophrenic house, composed of levels or pockets of energy that produce different feelings and atmospheres.

The house thinks it is a person almost – a person with an extremely weird sense of humour. The present occupants will suffer in more ways than one as a direct consequence.

Although there are many ways in which such a house may be cleared, it usually suffices simply to have animals around. However, because of the canine and feline sensitivity to atmosphere, and to the vibrations of colour, our pets can be used as vehicles for the transmutation of positive and extremely powerful healing energy that can bring about a complete transformation to the atmosphere in a very short time.

We must first of all try to understand that collectively the décor and colour arrangements of the house, psychically represent the character and psychological status of the family who live there.

Therefore, the subtle vibrations of the colour scheme of the house, that may already be producing some negative energy to begin with, may also have a profound effect upon the health of the family. This invisible and unwelcome visitor may also serve as a catalyst, thus causing the family to experience problems and difficulties one after the other, in a seemingly never-ending stream. The more negative the family becomes, the stronger and more powerful the house will grow, and so on.

This may sound like something straight from the pages of a horror story, but the truth is that this phenomenon is very often the primary cause of more family problems than we realize.

The more discord experienced by the family in a negatively charged atmosphere, the more likely they are to decorate the house in a colour scheme that corresponds directly to the negative feelings already experienced. Unless the atmosphere is transformed in a positive way, then the negative vibrations will be perpetuated by the already well established atmosphere.

Once you are certain that your house is the reason why things are going wrong for you, you may feel that the problem is in fact restricted to one particular room. In my experience the whole house is rarely implicated, so you should be able to isolate the areas responsible for the negative atmosphere.

By transforming the colour scheme of the house, and simply flooding it with brighter and more vibrant colours, you can encourage the healing process with, of course, the help of your dog or cat.

I must say though, that in the more severe cases of negative atmospheres more than one cat may be needed, as they tend not to be as psychically powerful as dogs in the cleansing process of a house. So, for this sort of healing application dogs are far more effective, and it is mostly when they are in a playful mood that they discharge most of their powerful healing energies. With this in mind, it is a good idea to target the most strongly affected room first of all. I would suggest that before you set about redecorating it, all your dog's toys and bowls be placed in there, allowing your canine to look upon that room as his or her own place, temporarily, at least, and to come and go as it pleases.

The colours we like are not always the colours that we should use. It is nearly always of great benefit here to break away completely from the colours we usually use, and to set about creating a colour scheme quite the opposite from our normal choice.

Yellows and pinks are quite stimulating colours and are extremely effective in clearing emotional garbage, and making the mind more relaxed and serene. Dogs tend to respond well to these two colours, and as well as stimulating the mental processes, yellow will encourage the self-healing process when there has been some depression.

Pastel shades are often more subtle, and can help to transform the look of a room in more ways than one. Try to work with these colours in varying shades and degrees, and if you feel that yellow will not work with pink, a little experimentation before you set about painting will help.

For the purpose of cleansing and creating a healing atmosphere, it certainly helps the process to encourage as much light into the room as possible. Perhaps a few mirrors strategically placed will help to create the desired illusion of brightness. This most certainly helps when there has been quite a lot of sickness in the home. Light created by the illusion of mirrors helps greatly to eliminate the negative and depressing vibrations of illness, thus precipitating the cleansing and healing process.

Allow your pet to be present during the colour transformation. Take an occasional break to stroke and play with it, allowing some interaction to take place.

Remember to experiment as much as possible, using as many different colours as you can, and allowing your personal tastes to take a break.

It is certainly a good idea to create a separate area in the house for your dog, especially as he is one of the family, and most probably an extremely important member of the family.

Although dogs enjoy interacting in family life, it is also advisable to allow them their own space if possible, where they can be alone with their thoughts, toys and other play things. Pale blues and pinks are extremely good colours with which to create your dog's area, and these hues also encourage its own personal energies.

Having transformed the colour and look of the negatively affected area of your home, open all the windows and allow as much fresh air in as possible. Burn some pleasant incense in the room, as this creates a beautiful, well-balanced atmosphere. Try to persuade your dog to stay in the room, and allow it to remain there overnight if possible. Watch exactly how it reacts to the colour and look of the room, and see how quickly it relaxes. This will give you some indication as to the success of the transformation. If your dog appears restless or agitated, it is more than likely responding to the dramatic psychic metamorphosis of the atmosphere, and it should settle down in a short time.

When there has been a complete metamorphosis of the atmosphere in the house you will see your dog roaming continually from room to room, as though searching for something. Dogs in fact are, by nature, curious creatures, whose senses are extremely acute, and always finely attuned to the surrounding atmosphere. If there is anything whatsoever still amiss your dog will most certainly know about.

Should you be a two or even a three-dog family, your house will be transformed in no time at all. Psychically dogs appear to work well in groups, and will not be phased by anything. Their collective energies can be quite powerful, and extremely effective when competing against an unpleasant atmosphere.

The single dog will nearly always approach a paranormal problem with great caution, and may sometimes even exhibit extreme fear. But the colour make-over of the house encourages the creatures inherent powerful healing energies, and do not forget that your dog not only has the power to heal you, but your house will also benefit from the process.

fourteen | Growing to Look Like Your Pet

The age-old belief that we grow to look like our pets is not as silly as it sounds – it is true!

To begin with, dogs are very much affected by their owner's personality, and to some degree they tend to emulate, in their own way, their owner's characteristics and personality traits. Although this may not be obvious to an onlooker, once the furry creature has established itself in the family it begins to exhibit strong feelings of adulation and admiration for its master and carer. The creature starts to psychically mimic its owner's personality, or what it sees as its owner's personality. It infiltrates the person's aura, gradually encouraging him or her to take on a subtle appearance of the furry creature itself. I know this will sound completely ridiculous, particularly to anyone who does not like, or own, animals. The animal lover, however, cannot deny that their pet to some greater or lesser degree influences them.

Our pets exert a great deal of mental control over us. In fact, living in close proximity to the family pet brings about a psychic metamorphosis of the owner's personality, until eventually he or she appears not only to walk like their dog, but they may even take on its stance and facial expressions. Furthermore, in my observations I have occasionally seen a man mimic his dog, from the walk to the wiggle – a mirror image almost of his canine friend!

A dog of slender nature with an elongated face is often seen to be accompanied by a man or woman of slender stature with an elongated face. Whether or not this is mere coincidence is a point in question.

Nevertheless, this very strange and at times hilarious phenomenon is often to be seen in the park or in the street. It is not uncommon to see an overweight Bulldog or Rotweiller accompanied by an overweight owner. Sometimes, one only sees the simliarities on a second, closer inspection.

A slow and lazy dog is nearly always accompanied by a similar owner. Likewise, the boisterous, full of energy dog is often to be found with a lively, full of energy owner. I must say though that there are exceptions to this rule, as some dogs possess far too much energy for their owners, who may be seen lagging tiredly behind their sprinting canine.

Cat owners do not escape the psychology of this phenomenon. The endearing qualities often seen in the family feline are nearly always mirrored in the human who is thought to be closest to it.

However, cats do not affect their owner's appearance in the same way as dogs do, but they most certainly mentally encourage changes in their human's personality and temperament. Like cats themselves, cat owners often fall into two categories: the one who remains calm and collected, even when in the midst of panic and chaos; and the worried, anxious, nervy one who lives perpetually on their nerves, and always under a veritable cloud of worry and stress.

Nevertheless, I have known some cat owners to almost take on the look of their cat. Beverly Nicholls, a well-known writer and lover of cats, now deceased, had, to my mind, an almost cat-like appearance. He obviously had an affinity with cats and wrote some extremely interesting pieces on the feline.

There are, of course, sometime limitations, I am not suggesting that the keeper of ferrets will come to look like the lithe creatures he or she keeps, or that the lizard fanatic will take on a reptilian nature – although there is always a possibility. Simply, that in the same way humans assimilate the behaviour of the circle of friends they spend their time with and look towards for advice and love, so they will emulate the pet they adore as much as a child of their own.

Cats and dogs have always played an extremely important part in the life of the human species. Dogs have always worked with and lived alongside man, and have evolved mentally and spiritually as a direct consequence. I am quite certain that our canines and felines are fully aware of the power they hold over humans, and I am convinced that they exploit this to the full. Our pets, in their own benefical way, are extremely manipulative, and far wiser and more intelligent than we give them credit for. It makes sense then, that if our pets have such a strong and powerful influence over our minds and psychic natures, then they have the ability to make us better when we are ill.

It is my belief, and a belief that is shared by an increasing number of people, that animals possess such metaphysical powers as were once possessed and used by our primitive ancestors. Although we have forgotten exactly how to use these powers, the Animal Kingdom has not. Because of the interactive natures of cats and dogs, these powers are somehow transmuted into potent healing forces that are able to affect the human organism in an extremely positive way. So, simply having animals around is very good for the psychological fitness of the human mind, and also for the health of the human body.

Whilst most dogs are territorial by nature, they are much more so where their owners are concerned, and literally weave a psychic veil over their human companion, in an effort to control and repel other furry creatures. This does not always work as people who have a strong liking for animals emit a powerful subtle scent, that informs other creatures that this human is an animal lover. While the person who does not relate to any animal other than their own pet dog will often find that other dogs will either avoid them completely, or perhaps show aggression towards them.

Although most canines, with the exception of a few, are quite tolerant of humans, they are extremely choosy, and are often very good judges of character. So, when a dog's will has been broken down through consistent acts of cruelty towards it, not only does it take a great deal of time and patience to rebuild its confidence in humans, but a lot of time needs to be spent healing the creature spiritually. When a dog has been cruelly treated its eyes reflect a deep disappointment that only the love from a new owner can heal.

There is no doubt about it – cats and dogs are characters, and the more one gets to know one's dog, the more this becomes a reality. Those who love cats and dogs tend to treat them like children, scolding them when they misbehave, cuddling them when they have been hurt, talking to them and laughing at them when they are in a playful mood. Our pets make us what they want us to be. They bring out in us those qualities that often lie deeply buried in our emotions.

ANIMALS HAVE THE POWER TO HEAL SIMPLY BY LOVING US.

fifteen | Animal Magic

Although this book is primarily an exploration of the healing abilities of cats and particularly dogs, this healing power is by no means restricted to the canine and feline worlds. On the contrary, a whole new concept in Animal Magic is opening up to us today, and as we enter the new millennium more and more people are developing the realization that animals are extremely special and vitally important to the spiritual and emotional evolution of mankind.

Animals too appear to be developing an awareness of humans, to the extent that many wild species are becoming quite tame, and are appearing to show very little fear of us. Next time you walk down the High Street just take a look at the way pigeons and sparrows walk about your feet, completely unperturbed by your presence. When you are sitting quietly in your garden see how close the birds come to you, again appearing almost oblivious to your presence.

Man's collective awareness is having a profound effect on

the wild animals and on nature. Although science informs us that the planet is in a sorry state due to our ignorance and abuse of it, there is an extremely significant spiritual epoch now beginning to dawn across the face of mankind.

The birds of the air, the fish of the oceans and the creatures of the fields and meadows are crying out with a desperate need to be allowed to share this life which man believes he has the sole monopoly on, and so therefore has exploited selfishly to the full.

All creatures, whether of the air, the land or the sea possess healing powers peculiar to their own species. Although most of these creatures will never have any contact with human life, their energies are continually discharged into the environment, precipitating a vibratory healing motion in the earth's surrounding atmosphere. Animals are the ambassadors of a much higher force than we will ever realize.

One of the cheekiest, most intelligent, and strongest healing birds is the blackbird, whose closeness to man has increased over the last 10 years or so. When this bird is in full song its aura becomes a beautiful display of pink, blue and yellow. Perched on the apex of a tall conifer tree, singing its heart out, the Blackbird is aglow with healing rays that can be seen psychically as bright sparks dancing in the air. Not only are these birds a delight to watch, but either listening to them singing or simply watching them play in the garden, creates a great deal of healing, which can be extremely effective when one is feeling under the weather.

Although you may not see many chimpanzees roaming the streets of Britain these creatures, which are so much like man, are veritable powerhouses of energy. The healing force is transmuted in their bodies in much the same way as in the human organism. In fact, the chimpanzee's subtle energies are organized in exactly the same way as man's, but with slight differences to the individual areas of the subtle anatomy. This indicates that the chimpanzee's consciousness has not quite developed to the level of its human brother, and it still uses faculties that man has long since forgotten about.

As a matter of fact, simply being with these creatures for a short while would be more than invigorating to a person recovering from illness. Chimps enjoy interacting with humans, and they derive a great deal of pleasure from human contact. In fact, a cuddle from a chimp is a huge experience in itself, and is like a tonic to the whole nervous system.

Chimps do enjoy so much being with humans, and they are also extremely tactile with no inhibitions. Although they can be extremely shy creatures, they can also exhibit a side to their nature that is extremely extrovert. Chimpanzees are by no means selfish creatures, and their human-like sensitivity allows them to exchange energies fairly freely.

The chimpanzee has the unusual ability to draw away negative energy from a human's nervous system, and the creature's presence is therefore extremely beneficial to anyone suffering from acute depression. I believe that the medical science of the future will employ the services of animals for the application of their healing powers. No longer then will animals be subjected to cruel tortures and experimentation in the name of medical science.

Simply by teaming the chimpanzee with the dolphin and the dog, the scientific minds of the future will discover an extremely powerful way of introducing healing to maladies of both the body and the mind.

Although dolphins have always demonstrated a great interest in the human species, and have always been recognized as extremely intelligent creatures, it is only in recent years that psychologists and other medical practitioners have actually involved them in the extremely specialized treatment of mentally handicapped children.

For some reason, unknown to conventional science, the dolphin is somehow able to interact with and work with children who are experiencing difficulties in either communicating with the external world, or who perhaps for some reason have closed off completely from it. The subtle energies of the dolphin appear to be able to penetrate through to the most 'difficult' mind, and to promote confidence and serenity.

The healing properties found in this most graceful creature are little understood by man, but are certainly thought to be almost magical in producing remarkable results where a tormented mind is in need of healing. In fact the dolphin appears to have an extremely cheeky and persuasive personality, and seems to almost know exactly what approach is needed. It is very careful around children, and because it possesses a playful nature children love to be around dolphins. They certainly enjoy interacting with humans, and have always been known for the interest they have shown in mankind. There are many stories of dolphins rescuing people who find themselves in difficulties at sea, and accounts of them either holding a drowning person above water as they guide them to land, or even leading a distressed ship through a storm to safety.

It is certainly not difficult to understand why some of the most prolific children's writers have focused their talents on animals, bringing their characters 'alive' and making them appear like animal-people. They obviously realized that animals do hold a great fascination for many people, young and old alike.

The magic of Rupert Bear, created by Mary Tourtel, was based, I am sure, on her experiences with animals and her knowledge of their abilities. The same most certainly must be said of Beatrix Potter, whose talents were able to bring alive so many creatures, from rabbits to hedgehogs and rats. In fact, no matter which book of animal tales one reads, they all have something very important in common, and that is that all the characters have intelligence and are able to communicate with speech.

In recent years Richard Adams brought alive a community of rabbits in *Watership Down*, a fascinating story that truly stirred one's emotions, leaving one with the disquieting feeling that rabbits certainly were able to talk and were just like people.

But it was Walt Disney who really brought animals alive visually. How many people can actually say, with hand on heart, that they have watched *Bambie* to its conclusion and remained dry-eyed? Even those who claim not to be fond of animals could not fail to be effected by the touching story of the orphaned deer, fighting for survival alone in the wild, without parents to care for it. There are, also, the ever popular Disney stories such as *101 Dalmatians*, *The Lady and the Tramp*, and *The Jungle Book* which tells the story of a young boy's interaction with various jungle animals.

There is no doubt about it, man has always wanted much more from the animal kingdom, and from his earliest days of childhood has always felt secure cuddling up to his Teddy Bear or his stuffed dog or cat.

Because man is so insecure he has always invented animals who can speak, love and care for him. Animals have always been a source of strength and friendship where the insecure man is concerned, fulfilling a part of his life that has always been empty and lacking.

There is no doubt that animals weave a definite kind of magic that is brought alive on the cinema screen. No matter what this magic is composed of, it most certainly has the power to heal the broken hearts of children, and sometimes adults too, by stirring the emotions and making them either laugh or cry.

The human fantasy about animals and their powers surely must have evolved from somewhere other than man's wishful thinking or needs. Maybe man and the Animal Kingdom share something, as do the two sides of one coin – man possesses a great need, and the Animal Kingdom has the power to satisfy that need.

Whatever it is that causes man's profound interest in animals, it just proves that animals, great and small, possess a very important kind of magic. In fact – *Animal Magic*.

sixteen | The Holy Presence

 If the purpose of man's sojourn in this world is that he may aspire to God-like status, then no doubt dogs have attained such exalted heights already.

All through this book I have said that our pets can be, and very often are, extremely manipulative, and most, if not all of them, do possess the knowledge of exactly what power they have over us. But in my exploration of the healing powers of animals, and in particular dogs, I have come to believe that they are the nomadic disciples of some holy power to which we are not privy – at least at present.

Losing a dog member of the family to many people is just like losing any other member. The grieving process is very often such that the statement 'No other dog will ever replace him. I'll never get another one', is said with feeling and finality. In fact, most dogs exhibit a huge presence around the home. Not only are they able to give that all-essential love to their owners, particularly when he or she is unwell, but the pet of the family somehow possesses the power to encourage that person to fight whatever malady has befallen them.

I heard about such a case from an elderly lady whose sister had died recently from a gangrenous condition that eventually spread throughout her whole body. The lady in question was in her early eighties, and had lived alone with her 14-year-old mongrel Michael, since her husband had died 10 years before.

It seems that, unknown to anyone, she had been desperately ill for at least two years, but had been afraid to seek medical attention for fear that her constant companion, Michael, would have to be put to sleep on her admittance to hospital. Sadly, Michael died suddenly of heart failure, allowing his owner to seek treatment in hospital, where she herself died only two days later.

This in fact is a classic case of the power our pets exercise over us by the love they encourage us to give them. They undoubtedly have an extremely powerful psychological effect upon our lives, and those who do not like animals are, sadly, greatly missing out on something quite wonderful.

Whatever magic it is that they are able to weave around us, dogs and cats know full well what they are doing. Their mischief, cheek and curiosity create an inimitable personality peculiar to that creature alone. It makes sense then that the owner of a cat or dog in whose relationship there is a very special bond will always be able to identify their pet from a line up of similar creatures.

There is no great mystery or surprise either in the story of the cat who disappeared just before its owners moved home from the north of England, to live in Scotland. This amazing pet somehow found them, after travelling the great distance on foot (or I should say on paw), to arrive miraculously at their front door, somewhat exhausted, two weeks later.

One elderly and overweight cat was apparently so fed up with being subjected to all sorts of (necessary) veterinary treatment that it left home, seemingly to punish its elderly owner. However, the cat returned six months later, half the size it had been, but apparently a lot healthier. Cat and owner now have an understanding – she always asks the feline's permission before taking him along to the vet, and she insists that her cat understands every word she is saying.

There is no doubt that the person who has been brought up with animals is emotionally different from the one who has not. Whether or not you accept the presence of a metaphysical healing force where animals are concerned matters very little. The truth is that animals great and small do pass on something to us, and this 'something', whatever one chooses to call it, is of great benefit to our emotional and mental equilibrium. The long-term effects of this on our physical health could be quite profound.

Catching sight of a rabbit, a squirrel, or even a weasel running across our path seems to cause the movement of chemicals in the brain, precipitating the emotions, and even the hardest of people cannot fail to be effected by such an experience.

It is one of life's great mysteries though how anyone can end the life of a wild creature in the name of sport, without the slightest feeling of guilt or sadness. Animals have to be so tolerant with us, and they cannot in any way protest about all the inhuman things that we impose upon them. Of one thing I am quite certain, and that is that even the most gentlest of animals are not given the opportunities that some of the wickedest, cruellest humans are given; and although the Animal Kingdom appears now to have a louder voice speaking on its behalf, the dreadful offences against them still continue.

Quite apart then from their wonderful and endearing value as family pets, dogs are in fact invaluable in many other ways: There are over 4,000 guide dogs for the blind in Britain, and over 100 extremely clever dogs trained especially to help the disabled around the home, and generally to make their lives a little easier. There are dogs trained to act as 'ears' for those whose hearing is impaired. They can fetch the post, bring in the milk, turn on the lights, and retrieve things from the fridge or cupboard. Dogs are now specially trained to search not only for drugs or bombs but also for missing or injured people and of course 'sniffer' dogs work with the police, army and rescue services.

The acute sensitivity possessed by both cats and dogs enables them to know in advance when there is going to be an earthquake, or even when a volcano is going to erupt. Of course, there is also the tradition of taking canaries down mine shafts to test for gas, or watching the behaviour animals show if a house is haunted.

Their psychic abilities enables both dogs and cats to measure the changes in the molecular structure of the atmosphere around them, enabling them to know about potentially devastating natural occurrences, often days in advance.

Dogs are not just cuddly ornamental creatures to have around the home, for they can also be useful in detecting an approaching epileptic fit, enabling the sufferer to take the appropriate measures long before it actually happens. Some dogs are now being trained especially to watch over severe epilepsy sufferers.

The auditory faculties of a cat are so acute that our human hearing is nothing by comparison. The cat can register sound frequencies up to 65khz, whereas we can only register frequencies up to 20khz. A cat's hearing is so sharp that it can home in to, and recognize, its owner's footsteps from several hundred feet away.

Dogs, it would seem, can register sounds of 35,000 vibrations per second, and a cat 25,000 vibrations per second, in comparison to a human's 20,000 per second.

Science today recognizes the importance and therapeutic value of having a pet, and it is now known that having a cat or dog around the home lessens one's susceptibility to most minor ailments such as headaches, depression, arthritis and even back-ache.

So a cuddle from your pet every day definitely keeps the doctor away. Tests have in fact shown that simply stroking your dog or cat helps to normalize blood pressure, and can also help to lower stress levels. As I have repeatedly pointed out in the pages of this book, so much more can be achieved simply by having animals around the home. How privileged we should be to share this planet with the Animal Kingdom.

Let us then look at the possibility that the Animal Kingdom as a whole is a constant reminder to us of all those things that we should be and all those things that one day we could be.

Remember also that the animals you have with you in your home are most certainly *Angels here on earth to help us, guide us and heal our wounds.*

Conclusion

The spiritual anatomy of animals is really not that far removed from man's, and although the powers of animals have been known by the ancients of the East for thousands of years, the Western world has only become aware of them in the last decade or so.

I said earlier on that – before the most rudimentary form of speech was evolved – many believe that man communicated his thoughts and feelings telepathically. Some wise writer on the subject once said, 'Speech was only developed so that man could tell lies.' Whether or not the latter is true, of one thing we can rest assured, animals do communicate without the intermediary of the senses. Unlike humans they speak in a language that is universal and most certainly not restricted to species, breed or geographical differences.

It is widely accepted that both dogs and cats possess a 'sixth' sense, and they are able to detect events well before they actually happen. Their acute senses are somehow so attuned to the surrounding atmosphere that they are able to register changes in the molecular structure around them. If they are able to use their sensitivity to this extent, then 'homing-in' on their owners would present no problem at all; thus it is quite easy to understand how a pet dog or cat knows when its master or mistress is feeling unwell. This would also explain why our pets gravitate towards us when we are feeling under the weather. Their natural instinct to care for us causes a release of an extremely subtle and yet powerful force that is immediately taken up by our nervous system.

Dogs in particular discharge this healing energy with the strong intention to make us well. The canine energy is completely different from that of the feline and somehow has a powerful psychological effect upon an invalid owner.

Modern day scientific studies have found that there is more to your pet's warm, reassuring fur than we previously thought. Connecting the dog or cat and their owner to an apparatus, sensitive enough to measure changes in the bodies of each, has shown that there is an exchange of energy when contact between the two is made.

Most dogs love to be around humans and possess the ability to encourage a sick or depressed person back to health. In fact, it was the knowledge of this that gave birth to the concept of P.A.T. dogs, that is Pets As Therapy. This popular practise of canine visitors for the elderly and the infirm can be seen now all over the country. A visit from a friendly Labrador can work wonders in encouraging a person to be released from the darkest depression.

However, it is not just depression that a friendly creature is able to help one with. Experiments have shown that regular cuddles or strokes can help to lower blood pressure and even ease a headache or migraine attack. Cats and dogs are thought to alleviate depression and ease acute back pain and even aid recovery from illness. There is very little doubt that being around animals is good for the psychological and physical health. Even the person who dislikes animals cannot fail to be effected when in their presence. The smallest of dogs can fill a room with love and healing, and their very presence in the home can eliminate depression or sadness.

Psychic Geography of the Body

Where does this healing force come from, and how exactly is it transmitted?

This perhaps is one of the most common questions that people ask, and one that can only be answered with some explanation of the psychic framework of both the animal and human body. A little understanding of the subtle anatomy will enable you take advantage of the full potential of your pet's healing power, so that you can gain greater control of it.

All that one needs to understand is that as well as a physical anatomy man also possesses a metaphysical anatomy. As the physical body requires wholesome and nourishing food to sustain it and maintain its health and wellbeing, so too does the metaphysical body require nutrients to maintain its vitality and equilibrium. The sustenance required with the latter though, originates with a different more subtle source, as I will now explain.

The cells, nerves, muscles and tissues of the physical anatomy acquire their vitality from the food we eat and the water we drink, and the entire organism is energized by the oxygen that we draw into our lungs. This oxygen is transported through the whole body via the blood, the flow of which is controlled by the heart. More than this takes place at a subtle level. For a moment, imagine that your physical body is replicated, and that this more spiritualized replica penetrates your physical body.

This metaphysical side of you is permeated by a network of subtle channels, along which energy flows from one part to another. You may understand these channels more easily as the 'Meridians' found in acupuncture, although in yoga they are referred to as 'Nadis', which simply translated means 'nerve'. The constant movement of energy along the meridians revitalizes the entire organism maintaining the health. Should you not treat your physical body properly, perhaps because of an unhealthy diet, or by allowing yourself to become stressed too often, the energy in the meridians congests and the flow is as a result restricted. This congestion has an effect upon the corresponding part of the physical anatomy. This causes the health of the person to breakdown and illness to manifest. A practitioner of acupuncture will locate the blockages, and at strategic points will insert fine needles to breakdown the congestion and aid the free flow of energy, thereby normalizing the movement of the force throughout the entire subtle anatomy. Once this process has been achieved health in the body is restored.

The movement of energy throughout the subtle anatomy is controlled by several powerpoints that serve as transformers. These powerpoints are believed to be connected to the major glands of the physical body via the meridians. Their primary function is to modify, transmute and distribute the subtle force around the body; the more constant the flow of energy the more vitality is allowed to remain, and a higher quality of life results.

The primary source of this energy is the sun, the rays from which pass into the food we eat and the water we drink. It is also carried into our bodies by the air we breathe which revitalizes our whole being. In the philosophical traditions of yoga the word 'Prana' is used to designate all energy in the universe. Roughly translated as the 'Life Force', this is believed to be the principle responsible for the integration of the cells into a whole. It is the binding force of the universe, and the energy responsible for the manifestation of life at all levels. The animal and the plant kingdoms draw this energy in from the air, and if it were not present death would occur.

Because this energy is used up quickly by the central nervous system, the process of respiration constantly renews the vitality, preventing the levels of energy from being depleted. In an unhealthy person these levels are not restored as efficiently as in a healthy person, and so the health continues to deteriorate as a direct consequence. However, some people are able to retain great streams of this vitality, and these individuals are usually good transmitters of the healing force. It is not necessary for such an individual to actually lay hands upon a sick person in order to pass on the healing power, for it is quite sufficient simply to be in their presence. I am quite sure that you have had the experience of being in the company of someone who has somehow made you feel uplifted, particularly when you have been feeling a little under the weather. It is not so much what they say or do that initiates the healing process as much as it is simply being in their presence. Animals in fact have the same effect on us without even trying.

The reason that animals are powerful healers is primarily due to their metaphysical structure and, particularly, the way in which it is arranged. They appear to possess more powerpoints than the human, so are therefore able to draw in and retain far more Universal Vitality. For example, where the subtle anatomy of the human possesses one powerpoint between the eyes, the dog has two, and in some cases three.

Your pet's network of subtle channels is also arranged differently, and although there are fewer channels, their arrangement is far more complex, primarily because of the levels of energy the creature's organism is able to retain.

As well as great stores of this potent healing force being contained in the animal's body, it also infuses the creature's aura and radiates approximately six inches from it, and in some cases extending up to 18 inches. The healing energy itself is an electro-magnetic force that can be extremely powerful, and can also be used to propel unwanted predators.

Cats and dogs are natural healers and delight in the fact that they possess the power to make us well. Although there is a great difference between the healing abilities of the cat and dog, they are equally as powerful where the process of healing is concerned.

Both cats and dogs are extremely psychic and both able to find their way back home from great distances. However, a cat's navigational system is similar to that of a bird's. It is somehow able to make a mental note of the position and angle of the sun in relation to where it is living, and is able to use these calculations to find its way back home when it gets lost. It does not have to be during the day either for it to be able to calculate its way home. Research has shown that a cat uses polarized light to get its bearings. And so even if the cat is taken blindfolded to the furthest part of the country, it will still be able to find its way back home.

As a result of a cat's sensitivity most of the homes situated on the slopes surrounding Mount Vesuvius keep cats as early warning systems. Although both dogs and cats are able to detect molecular changes in the atmosphere, the dog's sensitivity appears to be more refined and more able to work alongside humans. In fact, dogs are now being trained to perform all manner of things, from 'hearing' for the deaf, to 'seeing' for the blind. They can even collect the shopping from the local shop, and take the washing from the washing machine.

There is no doubt about it, a whole new concept of animal awareness is beginning to unfold today as the realization begins to dawn that we are sharing this planet with angels, and *not all angels have wings.*

It is believed that the only thing that sets man mentally apart from his animal friends is the fact that man possesses an intellect. In fact one writer once said: '*Man knows, the animal knows, but man knows that he knows because he has an intellect the animal does not.*'

I am not too certain whether the last statement made in this extremely profound precept is entirely true. I am quite sure that this remark depends upon exactly what definition one has of 'intellect'. Research has shown that evolution has caused the domestic animal to develop an intelligence that shows signs of a form of intellect. I am quite certain that animals are capable of developing greater things, and that in perhaps a thousand years they will have developed the ability to speak to us in a language that we will most definitely understand.

Glossary of Facts

Research in England, France and America has now lead veterinary science to conclude that having a dog or cat around the home is most definitely good for the health. In fact, an article published by the veterinary society in America stated that, 'Keeping a pet reduces the risk of heart disease, and makes you less prone to minor illnesses such as headaches, backache and even colds. It has also been scientifically proven that stroking a pet aids the relief of stress, and can reduce blood pressure and cholesterol levels.'

Some years ago a small booklet was published by a well-known animal food company exploring the powers of pets. The booklet highlighted the unusual powers our pets have over us, and offered scientific evidence of how the health benefits from having a furry creature around the home. This was not mere conjecture but evidence based on pure scientific facts. The progress of the health of some patients was carefully monitored after regular visits from P.A.T. dogs (Pets as Therapy), and the findings of the studies were quite remarkable. In some cases the psychological status of the patients improved by 100 per cent, particularly where those suffering from acute depression or even a terminal illness was concerned. In most of these cases improvement was spontaneous, and in others the process of recovery was gradual, but did continue until the patient was psychologically back to normal.

The Royal College of Veterinary surgeons now acknowledges the fact that animals do produce some positive changes in both the body and the mind of a person who is elderly or infirm. Although the reassuring warmth of the creature's fur obviously contributes to the whole healing process, research has shown that far more than this takes place upon contact with our pet. The furry creatures discharge a hormone that somehow causes the invalid's endorphins to be released. These are the body's own painkilling chemicals that also have the effect of creating feelings of euphoria. In other words, as well as creating its own healing force and contact with a sick person, the feline or canine also helps to initiate the self-healing process. Although science is able to monitor the animal's actual discharge of energy, as yet it does not fully understand why this process takes place, and what actually causes it. Initially the P.A.T. dog was thought to simply bring comfort because of it being cute and cuddly, but now opinions have most certainly changed. Much, much more takes place when the canine is in the presence of a sick person.

Nature has designed a special olfactory membrane to enable dogs and humans to smell things. However, in dogs this is considerably larger than in humans, which is probably the reason why dogs have longer noses than we do. This sensitive membrane enables the canine to recognize fragrances floating around on the air, then immediately passes on the information about the smell to the brain.

The sensitivity of dogs is now being used to smell for cancer in the bodies of humans. In 1994 Tallahassee dermatologist Armond Cognetta, M.D, a pioneering researcher studying dogs' potential to detect skin cancer, completely changed the mind of one sufferer. After numerous tests, doctors assured Natalie Tyler that the blemish on her shoulder was nothing to worry about, even though it continued to grow. Natalie's sister eventually persuaded her to consult Doctor Cognetta who introduced her to two dogs, a Schnauzer named George and a Golden Labrador called Breeze. These were in fact champion canine sniffers owned and trained by Duane Pickel. After only one meeting the two dogs were able to sniff and pinpoint the offending lesion on her shoulder. As the two dogs had never been wrong in their 'diagnosis', Doctor Cognetta advised Natalie Tyler to have the mark immediately removed. After 15 years with the mark on her shoulder, it was removed. The dogs had been correct, the mark was a malignant melanoma. Thanks to George and Breeze Natalie's life was saved. Although presently only in its pioneering stages, dog sniffing will be an integral part of diagnostic medicine in the future.

Dogs have also been found to calm the anxieties of Alzheimer sufferers. Experiments carried out at the School of Veterinary Medicine's Center for Animal Society, University of California, Davis, concluded that Alzheimer's patients were less aggressive and anxious when they were accompanied by a dog they were fond of. In fact, Lynette Hart, Ph.D., the Center's director, said that 'Animals have a normalizing effect on the behaviour of someone with Alzheimer's.' It would appear that this animal therapy is not in any way limited to dogs or cats. On the contrary, all animals whether finned or furred somehow have a remarkable effect upon Alzheimer sufferers. 'Pets are like fur-covered pressure-relief valves that allow us to decompress,' remarked one therapist at the Center.

Although it is fairly common knowledge that cats can see better in the dark than we can, research has shown that the images they perceive are not very clear. Cats' eyes are in fact anatomically similar to ours and according to veterinary textbooks possess two different types of receptor cells – cones and rods, just like humans. According to the experts 'cones' aid resolution and mean that the vision can be clearly focused to enable us to see objects, whilst 'rods' aid our night vision.

Although cat's eyes have more rods than humans, they do possess fewer cones, so whilst they can see better in the dark than humans, their vision is not all that clear!

A dog's hearing is capable of detecting sounds of 35,000 vibrations per second, a cat's hearing 25,000 vibrations per second, and a man's a mere 20,000 vibrations per second. This means that your dog is able to hear you coming down the street, and in nearly all cases is able to identify your footsteps and even the sound of your car engine. We often underestimate the powers of our pets and nearly always take their abilities for granted. Although a cat's hearing is not quite as acute as a dog's, it is still capable of detecting sounds that a dog cannot.

Ever since I can remember there was always a dog in my home. In fact, whilst I love and respect all animals, dogs are closer to my heart than any other animal. It was my deep interest in the Animal Kingdom as a whole that led me to collate the information in this book. The scientific facts and the observations I have made over the years will hopefully leave no doubt in your mind as to the extraordinary healing powers of animals. If you are one of those people who simply do not like animals at all then I am quite certain that you will completely disregard the subject matter of this book as fanciful and far-fetched. All that I can say is that all the facts are there; science is now beginning to change its previous ideas to reach new conclusions about the effects animals have upon our lives. Please do not dismiss the subject matter on one reading alone. Read it again when you have had time to digest the contents.

Concluding Thoughts

Animals play a much greater part than we realize in the spiritual evolution of mankind. I would go as far as saying that we could not live on a planet devoid of animal life, for they somehow promote and sustain the emotional, mental and spiritual equilibrium of our collective lives on this planet. The healing abilities of the animal kingdom cover an incredibly broad spectrum, from the faithful canine companion of the housebound pensioner, to the early morning birdsong that wakens us on a beautiful summer morning.

Pet healing is by no means a new concept, and it is known that the ancient Greeks encouraged the incurably ill to take a horseback ride to raise their spirits. Seventeenth century monasteries in England used cats and dogs to calm the mentally ill, and the residents of the monastic asylums would very often live their lives alongside canine and feline carers. Veterans of both World Wars would often receive pet therapy in hospital to aid their recovery from fatigue, known today as Post-Traumatic Stress Disorder.

Whilst I have always been a dog lover recently I became acquainted with an elderly Siamese pussycat called 'Suki'. When I am feeling a little depressed or perhaps under the weather she seems to know exactly what is wrong and endeavours to reassure and heal me. Although Suki is thirteen years old she still possesses extremely powerful energies but will only pass these on when there is a great need. It is often the case that the more mature creature only releases their healing energies carefully, almost in relation to the need of the person. This is not the case with the younger canine or feline who tends to be quite generous when discharging their energies into the surrounding atmosphere.

I, for one, feel so much better after a cuddle from a furry creature and can highly recommend such indulgences as an incredibly effective tonic particularly when one is feeling depressed. One Alzheimer's patient became so agitated and disturbed that it took Zoe a black Labrador to calm him down. The two became almost inseparable and there are even signs the sufferer's periods of agitation are decreasing in frequency.

Cruelty to animals is perhaps one of the worst and most unacceptable evils in the world today. How anyone can inflict pain upon a defenceless creature escapes me, and when we see how some nations demonstrate cruelty towards certain creature without any signs of remorse or conscience, we can see an incredible flaw in the spiritual nature of the nation as a whole. Fox hunting and hare coursing are perhaps two of the most despicable practises that are still regarded as 'sports' and which are also a sad reflection of the practitioner's lack of emotion and sensitivity. I must conclude this book with a piece of prose called 'The Hunt' which I wrote some years ago:

The Hunt

The early morning mist rises with shame
to reveal the flash of crimson coats.
No idle chatter from the hunters' lips
can conceal the deathly smiles,
nor magic away the guilt that is yet to come,
but even now is felt.

Excited hounds, hungry yet fed,
filled with eagerness for the chase,
mingle with impatient horses
whose frozen breath disappears with the rising mist, but still
the guilt of the hunters' deathly smiles remain.
Already the blood of the hunted flows,
but only in the minds of the hunters,
as they rub the cold from their frosty hands
and don their caps with pride.

The misty sky reveals a curious sun,
who peeps slyly, then retreats with shame,
as the signal is given and the hunt begins,
but for the hunted it is already over.
A wide-eyed creature stares from the safety of the hedge,
but its safety is soon to be broken
by the crimson coats, and howling dogs,
sounding horns, and horses at a gallop,
but led by the hunters' deathly smiles.

Confusion! And with hesitation,
the gentle creature surrenders.
Alas! no prisoners taken in this gruesome war,
as a curious sun peeps once again,
and the crimson coats congratulate each other
with outstretched hands; but the hunters' deathly smiles
slowly disappear, and the crimson coats
turn to coats of bloody shame...
...The journey home is always dark
but only in the minds of the hunters.